Clean up your financial problems with

HOT (broke) MESSES

"It's impossible to take the personal out of personal finance. Getting out of debt and learning how to live a financially stable life is not an easy thing. I can attest to that. I'm still a work in progress. But this book isn't just about me. I spoke to a number of experts to get tips not only for myself but for you."

—Nancy Trejos

- **Tracking finances:** Get great—and *free*—online budgeting tools.
- **Clothing shopping:** Score fabulous deals on the items you really want.
- **Credit card debt:** Find out how to avoid it *and* the best ways to pay off the debt you already have.
- **How to stay stunning on the cheap:** Discover when to skimp and when to spend.
- **Fun on a budget:** Learn how to save money whether you're entertaining at home or out with friends.
- **Car shopping:** Keep clear of costly mistakes.

and much, much more.

HOT (broke) MESSES

HOW TO HAVE YOUR LATTE AND DRINK iT TOO

NANCY TREJOS

BUSINESS PLUS

NEW YORK   BOSTON

Business Plus
Hachette Book Group
237 Park Avenue
New York, NY 10017
www.HachetteBookGroup.com

Business Plus is an imprint of Grand Central Publishing.
The Business Plus name and logo are trademarks of Hachette Book Group, Inc.

Printed in the United States of America
First Edition: May 2010

10 9 8 7 6 5 4 3 2 1

Library of Congress Cataloging-in-Publication Data
Trejos, Nancy.
   Hot (broke) messes : how to have your latte and
drink it too / Nancy Trejos. — 1st ed.
       p. cm.
   ISBN 978-0-446-55542-5
   1. Bankruptcy.   2. Debtor and creditor.   3. Compulsive
shopping.   4. Finance, Personal.   I. Title.

HG3761.T74 2010
332.024'02 — dc22

                                        2009027278

To my parents, Jose and Maria, Papi y Mami,
for always loving me, despite my flaws.

acknowledgments

Writing a book is like what I imagine a pregnancy would be like: You don't sleep well, you gain weight, you cry a lot, and you constantly worry that there will be something wrong with the final product. I would not have gotten through it had it not been for a number of wonderful, supportive, talented people.

I cannot take credit for coming up with the premise for this book. That credit goes to my former editor Steven Levingston. I turned to him during one of my darkest periods. He listened patiently, then surprised me by declaring that he thought I had the beginnings of a book. Without him, I would never have had the confidence to write a proposal. He wouldn't let me give up on this project. Steve, thank you for being an amazing editor, cheerleader, and friend.

Ilana Ozernoy, who has her own book coming out, provided constant encouragement and even found me an agent. To that wonderful agent, Robert Guinsler, a special thanks to you for your tenacious support. It was a nerve-wracking process, but with you guiding me, I knew it would all be okay. To my editor, Tracy Martin, for being so enthusiastic about this idea. You made this book much better with your skillful editing.

I would not have gotten this far in journalism had it not been for Benjamin C. Bradlee, Barbara Feinman Todd, and Ted Gup. Thank you for your support.

To my editors at the *Washington Post*, especially Sandy Sugawara and Gregory Schneider, for giving me time to write. I've spent most of my adult life at the *Post* and have had a number of other great editors. I am indebted to all of them for making me a much better writer and reporter.

I am especially grateful to all the people who took the time to read chapters of this book: Kay Robinson, Delphine Schrank, Daphne Benoit, Elham Dehbozorgi, Eric Lipton, Amit Paley, Zachary Goldfarb, Annie Gowen, David Cho, and Richard Engel. Your editing and input made a huge difference.

A special thanks to Richard. You always encourage me to take risks with my writing. Your advice, support, and friendship have meant so much to me.

To the Ontario Road Crew: Daphne, Elham, Eric, and Kavitha Babu. Irene Haggarty and Roy Magsisi, whom I grew up with in Queens, are also now in that crew. You are like family to me. Many, many thanks for getting me through the meltdowns, for always making me laugh, for cooking me wonderful meals, and for caring so much. I love you all, and I look forward to many more family meals together.

I am lucky to have befriended several other beautiful, smart, funny, and talented women in D.C. Thanks to Jay Newton-Small, Lizzie O'Leary, Christina Sevilla, Liz Lynch, and Christina Davidson. Kay, you are one of the wisest women I have ever met.

To my college crew: Mitch Rubin, Kristin Cohen, Deirdre Davidson, Doug Smith, Nick Singhvi, and Kathleen Miller. I'm glad we're all still in each other's lives.

To the Mezee, for all the advice on writing, love, and life.

The *Post*, like any newsroom, can sometimes be a tense place. How could it not? We're always on deadline. But I've managed to meet several people who have actually made going to the office much more fun. Some of you have left, but many of you, I'm happy to say, are still around. You have all been wonderful colleagues and, more important, dear friends. Thanks to Allan Lengel, who taught me that my self-esteem should not depend on what page a story runs on. To Keith Richburg, for making sure I had what every woman going through a breakup needs: wine, ice cream—and a Knight in Shining Armor. To Emily Wax and Justin Blum, members of the original "Oh No School of Driving Club." To Tony Faiola for making me laugh uncontrollably every time I hang out with him. To my fellow Colombian, Ernesto Londoño. And to Amit Paley, for always reminding me to "pull it together."

One good thing came out of the global financial crisis: I bonded with my colleagues on the *Post*'s Financial staff. I look forward to many more happy hours and lunches with Zach, Terri Rupar, Kendra Marr, Dina ElBoghdady, David Cho, Neil Irwin, and others on the staff.

To my other DC friends, Steve Rochlin, Tom and Gretchen Toles, and Bryan Greene, you guys rock.

Thanks to my financial advisor, Christine Parker, for setting me on the right path.

And thanks to all the people who were willing to share

their stories with me on the pages of the *Washington Post* and of this book. It takes a lot of courage to open up like that.

Most important, thank you so much to my family. Even in my darkest moments, I knew that you would still love me. I'm sorry I have not been around much all these years. I hope you realize that I respect and love you all. Thank you to Lucy and Danny for being wonderful siblings, to my beautiful nephews Edwin Jr. and Anthony, and to Edwin Sr., the best brother-in-law anyone can ask for. Thanks to my half brother Humberto, who welcomed me into his home even though he had never met me before.

And finally, a very special thank you to my parents, Jose and Maria. I have not always been the best daughter to you. I will always regret that. But you have always been the best parents to me. I will always be grateful for that. I admire both of you. What you have accomplished in your lives is unbelievable. I hope someday you will be as proud of me as I am of you. Mami y papi, I love you from the bottom of my heart.

contents

author's note

This book was not intended to be a memoir, but I soon realized that it is impossible to completely take the personal out of personal finance.

We all have relationships with money, good or bad. And those relationships start when we are young, living in our parents' homes. That's why I ended up writing so much about my family.

Money is what drove my parents to leave their homelands—Colombia in my father's case, Ecuador in my mother's—for the United States. As immigrants who knew very little English and had no college degrees, their earning potential was low. But they worked hard—my dad served food in a hospital cafeteria, my mom cleaned apartments and offices—spent little on themselves, and saved a lot of money.

They eventually achieved much of their American Dream: They bought a home in Queens, New York, and had three children, of which I am the youngest. They watched me graduate from Georgetown University in Washington, DC. They watched my sister get married and buy a house. They now spend much of their free time with my sister's two beautiful sons.

Unfortunately, I have not lived in my parents' home since I was seventeen. And because I knew little about finances when I moved to Georgetown University's campus, I got myself into trouble. In some ways, I feel that I have kept my parents from fully achieving their American Dream. They wanted their children to get married, own homes, and be financially stable. I have yet to achieve that. However, I am trying, and this book chronicles my attempts to do so. But this book is not just about me. I spoke to a number of experts to get tips not only for myself but also for you.

I also interviewed several other people around my age—many of them friends—who have either gone through financial turmoil or figured out ways to avoid it. In many cases their real names are used. In some cases, their real names are not used because they asked me not to.

Getting out of debt and learning how to live a financially stable life is not an easy task. I can attest to that. I'm still a work in progress. But I hope this book gives you some useful tips, and a whole lot of inspiration.

HOT
(broke)
MESSES

one
life in dc, as in debt city

I
t had been days, maybe even weeks, since I had logged on to Bank of America's website to see how much money was in my checking account.

It was June 2008 and I had spent most of the week talking to compulsive shoppers, hearing in excruciating detail how they ran up their credit card bills because they simply had to have that pair of Jimmy Choos to make them feel taller and sexier.

No, I was not doing this for fun. This was my job. I was the personal finance writer for the *Washington Post*, which meant that I had to write about how people spend, invest, save—or don't save—their money.

That day, I had interviewed a woman in California who had to seek therapy to deal with her shopping addiction. She had tens of thousands of dollars in credit card debt, brought on by twenty-two years of ferocious shopping. Her story terrified me. I realized then that I had been neglecting my own finances for far too long. On my desk at home was a pile of unopened bills. It was finally time to open them, I told myself.

I decided to stay in that night, which is rare for me. I got to my apartment building in Adams Morgan, home to the young and the hip of Washington, DC. Instead of heading straight to the elevator, as I often do, I walked over to my mailbox. When I opened it, it was stuffed with envelopes from people and companies I didn't want to deal with: Bank of America, HSBC auto loans, my podiatrist, Sallie Mae.

When I walked into my cozy one-bedroom apartment, I dropped my purse on a chair, sat at my table, and contemplated opening a bottle of wine. No, I told myself. I had to do this sober. I didn't want to turn into a drunken, sobbing mess. I had to work the next day. I slowly opened each envelope. Due to HSBC: $293.28. Due to Sallie Mae: $98. Due to Dr. Osterman, the podiatrist who treated a stress fracture in my left foot: $329. My stomach started hurting. My face got flushed. Suddenly, I felt like I was having a panic attack. I switched on my laptop and logged on to Bank of America's website.

Sure enough, what I saw did not make me happy. My rent was due in a few days. So was my car payment. I had enough to cover it. But I had also just sent out several checks to pay off various medical bills. I knew that on my modest journalist's salary, I would have no money left over to eat or even take the bus to work. And my next paycheck was a full ten days away. I was, by many definitions, broke. A broke personal finance writer. I burst into tears. There I was—a sober, sobbing mess.

I went to bed around 1:00 a.m. and tossed and turned. I thought about ways to make some extra cash. Could I find some freelancing gigs? Maybe, but that would not take care of my immediate needs. Could I take money out of my 401(k) retirement account? Perhaps, but...after a rocky few days in the stock market, I had probably lost a lot of money and would not even have enough to cover my debt. Plus, I was not even sure my employer would let me take out money. Could I sell off some clothing or computer equipment on eBay? Sure, but do I really have anything worth much? I surveyed my apartment and realized the only items of any value were my laptop and a tin, five-foot-tall Knight in Shining Armor that one of my best friends had bought me after my last breakup. ("This is the only boyfriend who will never leave you," Keith had said, as he shoved the knight into my silver Beetle after buying it at a flea market in Capitol Hill.)

I knew what I had to do. I could think of no other option. The next morning, I walked to work instead of taking the bus. I spent the first fifteen minutes practicing my speech to my mother. I finally dialed my parents' home phone in Queens, New York. My mother answered.

"Hola mami," I said in Spanish. She grew up in Ecuador and is more comfortable speaking in her native language.

"Hola mami," she said. She likes calling me that too. When I say it, I use it literally to mean "mother." When she says it, she uses it loosely to mean "dear."

"Que milagro," she said, which means "What a miracle." She was surprised to hear from me on a weekday morning. Usually we talk on Sunday evenings. Actually, she often says this at the beginning of our once-a-week phone calls. It's her way of reminding me that I don't call her enough.

"Um," I started. I told her about my medical bills, my car payment, my rent. Then, I told her I was out of money.

It took her a moment to say something. "How much do you need?" she asked.

I could tell she was disappointed. She and my father, who grew up in Colombia, never made it past high school and worked jobs that required manual labor. They had always dreamed of their children getting college degrees. Of their three children, I was the only one who did. I was also the only one with a career. My sister was a stay-at-home mom and my brother was unemployed. I was supposed to be the independent one. The one who made it. I'm the one she brags about to her siblings and neighbors. What she never tells them is that despite the fact that I was valedictorian of my high school, graduated from college, and went on to work at one of the best newspapers in the country, I am actually a mess. How many times had she told me not to squander away all my money? How many times had she scolded me for vacationing overseas too much? How many times had she looked at my closet in disbelief at the number of little black dresses I owned?

"A thousand dollars," I told her. I could have used more, but I couldn't bring myself to ask for it.

"Talk to your father," she said. She covered the receiver. I could tell they were having a conversation about me, but I couldn't make out the words.

Papi got on the phone. He didn't say hello. He got right down to business. "What is your mailing address?"

I was standing in front of the *Post*'s headquarters downtown, not far from the White House. At seventy-nine, my dad's hearing was not all that great, so he asked me to repeat my address several times. I did, very loudly.

"Ene Dobleoo, Ene Dobleoo," I kept shouting into the phone, as my colleagues walked past me and waved hello. That's how you say the letters *NW* in Spanish, which have to go after my street number because I live in Northwest DC. It took him a while to get it. "Ohhh, Northwest," he finally said in English.

"I'm so sorry I am doing this," I said once he had jotted everything down. I started crying, out of guilt and embarrassment. I moved away from the entrance so the people walking into the building would not see me in tears.

"Don't worry," he said. "This is what we are here for. There's no need to explain. You know what you're doing."

Did I really know what I was doing? No. For much of my adult life, when it came to money, I never seemed to do anything right. Yet when I borrowed money from my parents, I was a personal finance writer for one of the most respected newspapers in the country. I was writing about people in debt. I was writing about people going bankrupt. I was interviewing experts, then offering tips on how people could fix their finances, on how they could avoid getting into situations like the one I was in. I was spending most of my time tending to my readers, and little time tending to myself.

When it came to my own personal finance, I was basing my decisions on the personal, not the financial, part of it. I have made pretty much every personal finance mistake you can make. I got my first credit card in college. It didn't take long for me to max it out. That was the beginning of a string of errors.

Here are a few others: In January 2005, when I was twenty-eight, I bought an overpriced condo during the height of the real estate boom with my then-boyfriend, later my fiancé, and then had to sell it at a loss two years later after we broke up. When I turned thirty, I bought a Volkswagen Beetle that I really couldn't afford because I got sick of my old car and wanted to drive around in something cute. Now I hardly drive it and can't sell it for what I owe the bank. After another bad breakup in April 2007, I blew all sorts of cash on a crazy trip through California (I called it the Trejos Recovery Tour of 2007). I rented a convertible and drove up the Pacific Coast Highway, staying at nice hotels, getting spa treatments, and ordering but not actually eating fancy meals along the way.

Once I got off the phone with my parents, I asked myself: How had I become such a personal finance mess? My parents were good with money. They counted every penny, and made every penny count. Why had I not figured out how to be like them?

But the truth is: Few people of my generation are like them.

I am thirty-two years old as I write this. For the most part, people of my generation grew up in times of economic prosperity. We were children of the "Greed Is Good" era of the 1980s. We watched young people get rich during the dot-com boom. We watched real estate values soar. We watched the Dow Jones Industrial Average hit record highs. We made celebrities our heroes. We made *Us Weekly* required reading and reality shows like *The Hills* required viewing because we wanted to know what the rich and the beautiful were wearing, where they were vacationing, where they were dining. We tried to emulate our heroes even if our bank accounts couldn't support that lifestyle. When our bank accounts failed us, the nation's credit card companies did not.

We fell into a state of denial about our finances. We would go to the ATM and hit no when asked if we wanted a copy for our records. We would wait days before opening our credit card statements. We became live-for-the-moment people, and our mantra was this: Spend now, deal with the consequences later.

Decades ago, it wasn't until one had a career, a spouse, even a child that credit cards entered the picture. For the last several years, once people turned eighteen, they were bombarded with card offers. College campuses became breeding grounds for new consumers of credit, with companies using free T-shirts, food, even iPods to entice potential debtors. That will all change in February 2010 when a new law that restricts marketing to college students goes into effect.

That's not to say that the credit card companies should take all the blame. We may be young, but we are old enough to make our own decisions. And we often don't make the right ones because we have no concept of long-term planning. Here's some evidence: In a 2008 Fidelity-commissioned survey of about 1,200 workers between the ages of twenty and forty, those people we would think of as members of Generation X and Generation Y, 51 percent

said managing everyday finances, making mortgage payments, and paying down credit card debt were higher
priorities than saving for retirement. When switching jobs,
40 percent cashed out their retirement accounts rather than
keep it in a savings plan. Why think ahead when many of
us are postponing marriage and children? We have only
ourselves to worry about, only ourselves on whom to
spend money.

Our parents and grandparents, on the other hand, had
more responsibilities at our age. They got married earlier
and had families to support. Their goal was job security.
When they landed good jobs—or good enough jobs—
they worked hard for their money, and they worked hard to
hold on to their money. They were frugal. They paid cash
for everything, or if they used credit, they paid it off right
away. They planned for their futures and their children's
futures.

We were too many decades removed from the Great
Depression to understand what it felt like to have to
scrounge for enough money to eat, to pay for housing, to
survive.

In late 2008, I got an e-mail from an eighty-one-year-
old former personal secretary to three members of Congress
asking me whether or not she should close an American
Express card account that she was no longer using. I called
her to discuss her situation. Helen Galanoplos told me how
the memories she had of the Great Depression got her into
the habit of immediately paying the balances off on her
two credit cards. "I remember how things were. I remember a little boy coming to my door every night begging for

food. I think it put a fear in me of large debt of any kind," she said.

As I talked to her, I thought: Why is she asking me for advice? She was in great shape. I was not.

Darin Pope, chief investment officer of United Advisors, a wealth management firm in New Jersey, summed it up well. Our parents, he said, "saw their parents go through the Depression and what that entails. The Depression Babies, they saw that and reacted to it. They would be more miserable spending money because they would be more anxious about it even though they could take that vacation 100 times over. We've done a 180 at this point. Now no one cares. They spend what they make today tomorrow....There's going to be a point when there's a generation that does less well."

That point arrived in 2008. After years of rapidly rising property values, people finally stopped buying houses and condos. Many of those who had already bought properties realized they couldn't afford them. Foreclosures soared. The stock market tanked, not just in America but all over the world. Investment banks, which had financed many of the mortgages that people could no longer afford, became extinct. Auto companies went bankrupt. The federal government was forced to bail out major financial institutions that drive our economy. Americans were in more credit card debt than ever, just as they were losing their homes and their jobs.

We were in the midst of the worst financial crisis since the Depression. We were in a recession.

Our parents lived frugally to make sure that their

children would have better lives. Sadly, many of us do not. As the recession got worse, people my age started realizing their mistakes. Many started paying down their debt and saving more. Spending frivolously was out. Being frugal was in.

But for many of us, it was too little too late. We have become the middle-class poor. We are Generation Debt.

•　•　•

I grew up in Queens surrounded by immigrant families. Most of my childhood was spent in Jackson Heights, also known as Little Colombia at the time. (It has become Little India and Little Pakistan with a sprinkle of Little Colombia of late.) We were a fifteen-minute subway ride to Manhattan, which is where my parents worked. My father, Jose Trejos, served food in the cafeteria of St. Luke's Roosevelt Hospital on the west side, where I and the two siblings I was raised with were born. My mother, Maria Trejos, cleaned Park Avenue apartments during the day and midtown Manhattan offices at night.

When they weren't working, they were perfectly happy staying in Queens. Manhattan was too expensive for them. We never went to Broadway shows. We never tried any of Manhattan's wonderful restaurants. We never went to any of its great boutiques.

My parents reasoned: Why leave Queens if we didn't have to? If we wanted to eat out, there was the Mark Twain Diner where you could get a cheeseburger with French fries for $5. Or the Chinese restaurant on Northern Boulevard that lacked ambience, but had very tasty boneless spare ribs for less than $10. If we wanted to splurge we could go to La Pequeña Colombia, one of the fancier of the many Colombian restaurants in our neighborhood, where the portions were so huge we could split one entrée between two of us.

There was a good reason for their frugality. Combined, my parents made about $60,000 a year and had to raise three children in one of the most expensive cities in the world while paying a mortgage. My father, the oldest of eight siblings, also had to send money to Colombia every month to take care of his parents and siblings, as well as two children from a previous marriage.

So it's no wonder that we didn't take big trips, that we ate at home every night except Sunday, and that our clothing came from JCPenney and our shoes from Payless. When I was a child, my mother, who had gone to a beautician school in Ecuador, would cut my hair. (She once gave me really short bangs. Oh, how embarrassing!) My parents never wasted anything. Every food item in the refrigerator had to be used in some dish. My packed lunch would often include a sandwich with the ends of the loaf of bread. If my dad noticed that the light in my bedroom was turned on when no one was in there, he would switch it off. To this day, my mom wears the same hot pink sweater with pandas on it that she has had since I was a teenager. The *Little Mermaid* bedspread I used in middle school is still on my childhood bed.

My parents did, however, splurge on important things. The public schools in our neighborhood were horrible, so they scrounged together some money and sent me to private Catholic schools. When it was time for me to choose a college, they didn't limit my choices to a public or local university close to home. I had a grade point average that exceeded 4.0 because I did so well in my honors courses. As much as they hated to see me leave our home, they wanted to reward me for my hard work and helped me pay for Georgetown University in DC.

Everything my parents did was for their children. They didn't want us to live like they had in their native homelands. During one of my visits to New York, I asked my mother why she was so frugal. "I don't buy anything I don't need," she said. "I don't buy clothes. For what? To keep in my closet? I don't go to parties. I don't go to restaurants all the time. I'd rather spend my money on my children and my grandchildren. You have to help them."

My parents are retired now. Through Social Security and pensions, they earn about as much as they did while working. My mom received extra money through a worker's compensation case. Their house is paid off. They have a home equity line of credit, which is covered by the rent they earn from their basement apartment. They have money saved up. They rarely use credit cards.

"It's about willpower. You have to be strong and learn how to live within your means," my mom told me.

My mother grew up on a farm in Ecuador. There were many nights when dinner consisted of slices of bananas mixed with rice.

My mother couldn't afford to go to college and not work full-time. At sixteen, she decided to leave her small town near the southern city of Cuenca without telling her parents. Ironically, she said it was her vanity that drove her.

"I had two dresses and one pair of shoes. I wore the same clothes all the time. I was ashamed. By then, I was starting to date. I said, 'I have to do something about this,'" she recalled.

So she moved from Cuenca to Quito, the capital of Ecuador, then to Guayaquil, another big city, in search of work. For four years, she tried different jobs at nursing homes and hospitals, even a mental ward once. Eventually she grew tired of that and convinced herself that she could do better in America. She saved enough money for a plane ticket to New York and took off in 1968, much to her parents' dismay.

It wasn't easy. She hardly knew English. She worked at nursing homes, in factories, cleaning people's homes. She bounced around from one apartment to another, living off the kindness of friends or renting tiny rooms here and there. She was sexually harassed countless times.

She met my father just a few months after arriving in America. He had already been in America for four years. They bonded over their similar backgrounds. My father had grown up in Pereira, a big city in the western part of Colombia. My grandfather worked odd jobs here and there—at a bakery or selling guns or anything else he could get his hands on. My grandmother made hundreds of empanadas each week. My dad's first job, at age six, was hawking those empanadas for a penny each in one of the city's main plazas. My dad went to school until age twelve. "I loved math. I loved school. I wanted to keep studying, but I needed to make money," he told me. "My family needed me. But I would have been a great student."

He carried bags for passengers at a train station. He sold popcorn, ice cream, and newspapers. At seventeen, he moved to Cali, a much larger city, and managed a billiards hall, becoming a minor local celebrity because of his pool-playing skills. He briefly joined the military before being married to the mother of his first two children for a short time.

Dissatisfied with the living he was eking out, and with violence spreading across his country, he decided to move to America. He arrived in 1964 with $135 in his wallet, no English-speaking skills, and no prospects for a job. He was thirty-five years old. He paid $50 a month to sleep on the living room floor of an acquaintance's apartment in Manhattan and worked in a nursing home. "It was a hard life but this is where the opportunities are," he said.

In 1968, he saw one of those opportunities in a movie theater. He was walking out of the theater when he spotted the pretty, spunky woman who would become my mom. She was with her cousin and her cousin's boyfriend. He decided to watch the movie a second time and took the seat next to her.

When it was over, he offered to take her and her companions to dinner. My mom didn't want to go. She thought he was too old for her—and she wasn't hungry. Her cousin's boyfriend, on the other hand, was very hungry and convinced her to accept my dad's invitation.

For the next few months, she repeatedly refused my father, but he kept showing up with flowers and food for her and her roommate. He eventually won her over with carnations and plantains. They got married in 1969. My brother, Daniel, and sister, Lucy, were born just over a year apart. I am the youngest of the three.

My parents hardly saw each other because of their work schedules.

My father would get up at 5:30 a.m. every weekday morning. He would always wear a collared shirt, dress pants, and a fedora, even though he was taking trays of food to patients' rooms all day long.

My mom would get us up at 7:00 a.m., feed us, walk us to school, then run off to her job cleaning apartments for wealthy lawyers and businessmen. Sometimes, if I was too sick to go to school or had a day off, she would take me with her. I remember one Park Avenue penthouse in particular. I was mesmerized by the size of the kitchen with its island in the center and two-door refrigerator. I was amazed that the master bedroom had a stationary bike in it. While my mom cleaned, I ran around from room to room. I was shocked at how many there were. Why couldn't we live this way?

On the days I was in school, my mom would make it back in time to pick me and my siblings up when classes were over. Then she would quickly make dinner. Like my dad, she would get dressed up for work even though she had to change into a uniform once she got there—never pants, always a dress or skirt and blouse, and high heels.

My mom would leave for her full-time job around 4:00 p.m. That's around the time my dad would get home, usually with a bag of M&M's or a Charms Blow Pop lollipop for each of us. Sometimes my parents would run into each other. Sometimes they wouldn't. My mom got off work around midnight or 1:00 a.m. Lucy, Danny, and I would often stay up late waiting for her. Mami would show up with a bag of donuts or McDonald's cheeseburgers for us. We would all eat together, then watch *Star Trek* before going to bed. We were exhausted in school but so grateful for the time we got to spend with our mom.

It was a tough life for my parents, but they say they wouldn't have done it any other way. Their American Dream was to raise children, own a home, and make sure their children eventually got married and owned their homes as well. They had no desire to travel, to go out to hip bars, or to follow the latest fashion trends.

Many years later, I concluded that I too had an American Dream.

A good friend made me realize what that dream was over dinner in a foreign city one night. His philosophy was this: Our lives are divided into parts. The first ten years don't really mean anything. We're children and we don't make any decisions of our own. The next five to eleven years, we are students. The five years after that are the screwing-around years. We don't really know what we want, so we try different things. The next forty-five years until we retire or die are what truly matter. That's when we define ourselves. That's really all the time we've got to be who we were meant to be in this world. So we have to make a choice. Are we spouses, who devote ourselves to raising children? Are we philanthropists, who spend all our time giving to others? Are we conquerors, who run organizations, companies, countries, etc.? Are we hedonists, who focus on accumulating wealth, traveling, and getting regular facials and pedicures? Or are we explorers, who spend our lives looking, not looking for something, but just looking?

I knew exactly what I was. I was an explorer. That was my American Dream. I was in no rush to settle down and raise children. I could have had that once. I spent five years with one of the sweetest men I will probably ever meet. He would open doors for me and constantly tell me how beautiful he thought I was. We got engaged when I was twenty-eight. But happiness eluded me. On our vacations, he had no desire to go anywhere but California, which is where his family lived. He had never left the country and didn't want to. He wanted to write beautiful stories, be a good husband and father, and eventually move back to his hometown. I felt smothered. I loved him but I didn't want the life he was offering me. I wanted to have a fulfilling career, to spend time with family and friends over good meals and cocktails, to see the world, to meet interesting people, to accessorize well, to have passionate love affairs, to read good books, to write. And I wanted to do it all without hurting myself or the people I love. It seemed so simple.

Except that it's not, because that kind of life can get expensive. So in my effort to achieve that dream, I was now living an American nightmare. I was living above my means.

I was living in debt.

two

the college years: keeping up with the jane hoyas

My whole family drove me 225 miles south to Georgetown University in our old Mitsubishi Gallant. The parking lot near my dorm was filled with shiny Mercedes Benzes and BMWs.

I was a seventeen-year-old carrying a suitcase stuffed with flannel shirts and jeans, a pair of Chuck Taylor's and a pair of Doc Martens that I had begged my mother to buy me. My wallet had a few hundred dollars in it, some of it savings from my summer job as a cashier at Woolworth's but most of it from my parents. Tuition, room and board, and all the fees were going to cost about $26,000 to $30,000 a year. I had received a partial scholarship and took out a couple of low-interest loans from Sallie Mae. My parents were picking up the rest of the tab. To cover my day-to-day expenses, I got a job under the federal work-study program as a chemistry lab assistant. One of my duties was carrying dry ice into the lab every Monday morning.

It didn't take me long to feel out of place. I had a New York accent, a shabby wardrobe, and little disposable income. Many of my classmates were trust fund babies, or at least acted as if they were. Some were the children of bank executives, members of Congress, business owners, ambassadors, and other diplomats. One of Diana Ross's daughters was a student. They were wannabe lawyers, investment bankers, hedge fund managers, diplomats, and politicians. We had names for the well-groomed, well-mannered, well-reared of Georgetown: Jane and Joe Hoyas. Jane and Joe wore J.Crew and Brooks Brothers, partied hard, and went to Europe or the Caribbean for spring break.

I dated around my first couple of years, mostly guys I met at the *Georgetown Voice*, the student newspaper where I was working. It was cub journalist-on-journalist dating, not unlike the real media world. (I would discover later that journalists often date each other, which is not always a good thing, because our profession attracts some commitment-phobic, career-driven types who are not always good with money.)

In my junior year, I started dating someone who was a year ahead of me and came from an affluent family. He was a student in the business school and knew exactly what he wanted to do: Something that involved helping people get rich. He was not materialistic. He was kind, loyal to his family and friends, and had a good sense of humor. But he had his finances in order and wanted to keep them that way.

On our first date, he asked me where I wanted to go to dinner. I really had a craving for a Subway sandwich.

"I am willing to buy you dinner anywhere and you want to go to Subway?" I recall him asking in disbelief.

"I just really like Subway," I said.

He obliged. That is, until our third date. From then on we

frequented restaurants around Georgetown. We didn't always go to fancy restaurants, but we did go to places where we could linger over decent salads or burgers. He knew that I didn't have much money, so he would pick up the tab.

When my boyfriend and I broke up after his graduation, I was well on my way into debt so that I could keep up with the rest of the Jane Hoyas. I had MBNA (now Bank of America) to thank for that. That credit card offer came not long after I arrived at Georgetown. I started dressing in nicer clothing, thanks to my new credit card. I bought CDs and drinks, thanks to my credit card. I became more of a Georgetown girl, thanks to my credit card. And I was hundreds of dollars in debt, thanks to my credit card. By my junior year I had a better-paying part-time job at the Associated Press, and much of my salary was going toward paying off my credit card.

I learned many things in college. I took classes on Russia's history and politics, on the politics of the Christian Right, on female writers of the nineteenth century. But not one class taught me about personal finance. No one told me to read the cardholder's agreement. No one told me that your 7 percent introductory interest rate could eventually go up substantially, making your minimum monthly payment suddenly seem much more difficult to manage. No one told me that taking cash advances would cost you even more because you would be borrowing at a higher interest rate.

Credit card companies got better at marketing to college students. In my day, we would get T-shirts for filling out a credit card application. Years later, students started getting free pizza, Potbelly's sandwiches, gift cards, or iPods from credit card issuers. Some companies even paid students to go around campus and convince their classmates to sign up for a card. "They've definitely gotten more creative," said Curtis Arnold, founder of CardRatings.com, which tracks the industry. In 2008, the U.S. Public Interest Research Group, which advocates for consumers, surveyed students at 40 colleges in 14 states. Seventy-six percent reported stopping at tables on campus to apply for cards, and nearly one-third were offered a free gift to sign up.

A credit card company spokesman pointed me to another survey conducted that same year. In a survey of 1,200 full-time undergraduates conducted on one hundred campuses, the marketing research firm Student Monitor found that the percentage of students with a credit card in their own name had decreased, from 46 percent in 2004 to 35 percent in 2008. Of those who had cards, 63 percent said they pay their balance in full each month. The 37 percent who did not carried an average balance of $452, a decrease from the previous year, the report said. Students had more student loan debt than credit card debt, the study pointed out.

The companies' tactics have worked. Nearly two in three students surveyed by U.S. PIRG said they had at least one credit card. Fifty-five percent of cardholding students said they used their card for day-to-day expenses. In a sign of how expensive a college education has become, 55 percent reported charging their books while nearly one-quarter said they pay their tuition with a card. On average, those freshmen whose parents were not helping them pay their bills had a balance of $1,301. Seniors were worse off. They had $2,623 in credit card debt.

Going Downhill

With so many college students graduating with tens of thousands of dollars in student loan debt, can you imagine what adding credit card debt can do to their financial stability?

"I've seen it too many times over the years," Arnold said. "It may start small but it's like a snowball going down a hill. Before you know it, halfway down the hill a year or two later, it gathers significant speed. That's when it's an 'on a path to destruction' kind of deal."

I started on that path in 1995, when I got my first credit card. Many of my ideas for stories come from what I've experienced, which is why, in April 2008, I decided to write about how today's college students were still falling into the credit card trap.

When I talked to Holly J., she was a nineteen-year-old sophomore majoring in government and politics at the University of Maryland in College Park. She had gotten her first credit card, a Bank of America Visa with a limit of $1,500, a year before. She nearly maxed it out just buying books, which cost about $500 each semester, and paying for utilities and food. She then opened a Dell card because she needed a laptop. Before she knew it, she was more than $2,000 in debt. "I just kept thinking it was just a little bit more that I was putting on and it would be easy to pay off," she said.

She soon realized that it's not so easy. To pay off her

debt, she got a job at the Gap, working fifteen hours a week and earning $7.75 an hour. "Now all my paychecks are going to the minimum balance of my cards," she said. "I don't know what to do."

She was trying to figure it out on her own. In fact, she told me about her credit card debt before she told her parents. "I don't want them to think I'm irresponsible. They'll only get mad," she said. "There are a lot of months where I have to borrow money from my parents. They don't understand why. They think I'm spending it on parties or clothes, but I'm really not."

I totally understood her point. I tried to hide my credit card debt from my parents as long as possible. I eventually fessed up while visiting them one weekend. They obviously weren't happy and advised me not to use my card anymore. But I was young and selfish and wanted to go to the Bahamas with my friends for spring break.

Having a credit card is not necessarily a bad thing, when you're mature and responsible enough to handle it, which I clearly was not when I got my first one.

"The danger is of course somebody who is going to say 'Oh I'll buy pizza for my friends,' 'I'll go shopping,' or 'I'll go on the ski trip.' That's the real risk," said Emily Peters, who up until taking another job in mid-2009, was a personal finance expert at Credit.com, which tracks the industry.

Given that there is such a risk, and that college students don't typically have a steady income stream, does it make sense for companies to hook them in so early?

Congress and President Barack Obama have said no. In May 2009, Obama signed a new law that would prevent credit card companies from marketing so aggressively on college campuses. Anyone under twenty-one cannot get a card unless he or she finds a cosigner or proves that he or she has the means to pay off the debt. Any increase in the credit limit would require written approval from the cosigner.

That law will go into effect in late February 2010, too late for the many college students who have already gotten into debt. They will have to find a way to undo the damage.

I talked to Holly again shortly after Obama signed the new law. She had undone the damage by asking her parents for help. They paid off one of her cards while she used her salary from the Gap to pay off two other cards. Unfortunately, she then spent a semester in London and racked up $1,500 in debt by shopping and going out.

"I wish I had just closed the account once it was paid off," she said.

The good news is, she's still young and has time to recover. But she'll have to start working on it right away.

If you too are a college student in debt, these tips, which I gathered from several experts, might help:

- *Go to a credit counselor.* There are many reputable credit counseling services that will help you by negotiating payment plans and lower interest rate payments with your lenders. But beware, because many fly-by-night debt consolidation companies have sprung up over the years. Make sure whatever credit counseling service you turn to is affiliated with the

National Foundation for Credit Counseling or the Association of Independent Consumer Credit Counseling Agencies. If they are charging you excessive fees or your payments aren't making it to your creditors, then there's something seriously wrong. Check with the Better Business Bureau, your state attorney general, and your local consumer protection agency to find out what complaints have been made against them.

- *Seek out university resources.* Find out if your school has any counselors who can help. Or ask a finance professor for advice. Many schools have started incorporating financial literacy into their curricula or freshman orientation. At George Mason University in Virginia, for instance, freshmen have to take Mason 101, a course on handling college life that includes a lesson on credit cards.
- *Turn to your parents.* I know it can be painful to admit your mistakes to your parents. But sometimes, it's necessary. If you simply can't make your payments on time, you might have to seek advice from Mom and Dad. They might not give you the money to pay off your card, but they can help you call your credit card issuer and negotiate a lower interest rate. "Whether college students realize it or not they're your best friend and your biggest advocate," said Susan Coleman, a finance professor at the University of Hartford's Barney School of Business. "Frequently when you're in over your head and you call your credit card company they will work with you. But college students...shouldn't

navigate those waters by themselves." If you're worried about their reaction, tell them how sorry you feel about it, how you want to learn from your mistakes, and how you want to become more responsible. (And please, mean it when you say it.)

- *Get a part-time job.* Not only will you make money but you will also show your parents that you are trying to get your finances in order. Make sure the money goes toward paying off your debt, not buying beer for your buddies.

I wish I had known to take these steps when I was Holly's age. Otherwise, the next chapter of this book and my life probably would not have happened.

three
oops!…i did it again, and again, and again

The summer of 1998 marked a first for me: The first time I lived alone. No longer was I at my parent's house, in a dorm, or in a group house with seven other people. I rented a studio apartment in Dupont Circle, a fun, largely gay neighborhood a few blocks away from the *Washington Post*, where I was working as an intern for the Metro section. Rumor has it that John F. Kennedy Jr. had once lived in my building. I never confirmed that, but I liked to mention it to friends who came to visit anyway.

I loved my neighborhood. A block away was a strip of restaurants and bars. I paid $650 a month for the studio, which I turned into a one-bedroom by sticking my futon in the large walk-in closet that separated the living room from the bathroom. I furnished it with some leftovers from the group house I had lived in during my senior year and a green velvet sofa bed that a professor had given me. The apartment was cute, but it had one flaw: roaches, formidable ones. "It wasn't the quantity of the roaches. It was the quality," my former college housemate Nick said when trying to describe them. In any case, it wasn't anything some Raid and a much-pleaded-for fumigation couldn't take care of.

I was willing to live with that so I could stay in DC and intern at the *Post*. The *Post*'s internship was one of the most sought after in the country. Sure, I deserved a spot in the internship class after running the *Georgetown Voice* and spending every weekend for two years working for the Associated Press. My AP job consisted of following President Bill Clinton around in his press pool when the real White House correspondents could not—or did not want to—and writing stories about anything interesting he said or did while playing golf or attending a party. Mostly, though, I owed my break to Benjamin C. Bradlee, the legendary former executive editor of the *Post* during Watergate. I took a seminar he taught at Georgetown during my senior year. Somehow, even though I showed up to class always looking sleepy because I was juggling the campus paper, my AP job, and a full course load, he liked me and encouraged me to apply to the *Post*. Thank God he did. Aside from being one of the best newspapers in the country, the *Post* was also paying its interns about $750 a week at the time, making it one of the best paid journalism internships.

I had to leave the *Post*—and that wonderful salary— after that summer because I had lined up a two-year internship with the *Los Angeles Times*. The work was great. The pay was not. The *Times* covered the rent for my studio apartment. It had a horrible Murphy bed that became a mirror when you pushed it into the wall. To make up for that design flaw, it had a fantastic balcony with a view of the Hollywood sign. Instead of a salary, I received a stipend of $250 a week. If it wasn't for my parents buying me a car for my graduation, I would not have been able to survive. I lived frugally, a word you don't normally associate with LA. It helped that I hardly knew anyone there. I hung out mostly with the other people in my internship program, but they too were making too little to hit the Sunset Strip all the time. I worked long hours because I wanted to write stories that were good enough for the *Post* to hire me back. Night after night, I would go home to watch a Blockbuster videotape and eat the same dinner—two flour tortillas with some shredded cheddar cheese sprinkled in between, microwaved for a few minutes.

Being a starving writer had some benefits: I lost all the weight I had gained in college from my many nights eating Domino's pizza and drinking Rolling Rock beer. But I had no disposable income and little savings, so when a tire went flat or another unexpected expense popped up, I would have to borrow money from my parents.

Fortunately, a year into the job, Richard Paxson, a now deceased editor I had worked with at the *Post*, called to ask if I would be interested in returning as a Metro section reporter. "Yes!" I immediately responded. I flew to DC for interviews. After a few hours of meeting one editor after another, he handed me a Post-it note and instructed me to write down my salary.

"I have a stipend, not a salary. I'm not sure what I make," I said, obviously lacking any negotiating skills.

"Just write down what you think you make," he said, looking amused.

I wrote down $27,000. He looked at it, chuckled, and said, "We can do better than that."

And they did: $46,000. I took the job on the spot.

I returned to the *Post* feeling triumphant. This was it, I told myself: The financial stability I had always wanted. I was earning nearly as much as my parents' combined salaries. I would not screw this up. I would be a successful female journalist in the most powerful city in the world working for one of the most influential newspapers in the country.

But I was twenty-two and impulsive. I had gotten used to a lifestyle I really could not afford. I liked to dress well, I liked to eat, I liked to drink, and I liked to socialize. The fact that I had some money made me want to spend it more. I figured I could afford anything because if I spent my paycheck, it didn't matter. I would have more money in two weeks. I would pay my rent on time, but I was once again using my credit card when I felt like buying a cute skirt from J.Crew or a hat from one of my favorite boutiques. I was saving nothing. I didn't even start a 401(k) retirement savings plan when I became eligible for one. I wasn't thinking about the future. I was barely thinking about the present.

For much of my twenties, I felt like every time I made progress financially, something would set me back so that I had to sprint again to get to where I started. I never got beyond that point.

There's a term for this. It's called the hedonistic treadmill. This is the idea that when you get what you want, you get used to it, and then you want more.

"We adjust to whatever our situation is. So when we move up in the world, obtain a higher salary for example, we adjust to that level of salary. $100,000 on the first day you make it isn't worth as much as a year later. To stay happy, you have to always have a little more to counteract this downward adaptive trend. Hence the treadmill—to stay in the same place, you have to keep walking," said Matt Wallaert, a behavioral psychologist at Thrive, a free online personal financial advisory service for people in their twenties and thirties. "People say I'm making $30,000 now and I'll be making $1 million later. The problem is, when you're making $1 million, you spend like you have $1 billion and you're paying off your debt at the same time."

I kept getting raises at the *Post*. Twice a year, actually. Every time I got more money, I told myself I would pay off my debt and become financially stable. But I didn't. I just kept spending. I did this to boost my self-esteem, which for one reason or another was low at the time. It is something I have struggled with all my life. I had been anorexic and bulimic as a teenager and never fully recovered. I have never been happy with my weight, so when I found an outfit that made me look pretty and thin, I got happy. I was addicted to that emotional high. I was sabotaging myself.

Running in Place

And then, of course, I fell in love. Once, twice, it doesn't matter. Add romantic notions of coupledom to selfish hedonism and a dysfunctional relationship with money and you get a toxic financial stew.

I met Live-in Boyfriend #1 when I was twenty-three. He was four years older. The *Post* had flown him in from

California for a job interview. My friend Darryl was charged with taking him out to dinner and invited me along. Never one to turn down a free meal, I consented. The dinner was pleasant. Live-in Boyfriend #1 seemed nice — shy, actually. I sort of forgot about him until eight months later, when I ran into him in the *Post*'s newsroom.

"I had dinner with you a few months ago, didn't I?" I asked.

He smiled. "Yes. I just started this week," he said.

We started dating soon after. Almost a year later, I moved into his one-bedroom apartment near the *Post*. Although my *Post* salary had increased considerably, I was still making less money than Live-in Boyfriend #1. He offered to cover the rent if I took care of utilities, which left me with quite a shopping budget. Instead of paying off my credit card debt, I used my disposable income to shop. I recall going through a suits phase. Journalists don't dress up very often. Some people show up in jeans every day. For some reason, I decided I liked the way I looked in suits. Before I knew it, I had bought half a dozen of them. They weren't each terribly expensive, but together they cost me about $1,500. It was a complete waste of money.

I made my biggest financial mistake with Live-in Boy-friend #1. My parents had always pushed the idea that you haven't made it in America until you've bought property. They kept telling me that Live-in Boyfriend #1 and I were throwing away our money in rent. If we bought a home, all our money would go toward something we owned. Plus, we would get tax breaks. In January 2005, we finally gave in. We settled on a brand new $375,000 one-bedroom loft-

like condo in a DC neighborhood made hip by the opening of a Whole Foods. My mom gave us enough money for
a 10 percent down payment. Our monthly mortgage was
$2,100, a substantial increase from the $1,200 we—well,
Live-in Boyfriend #1—had been paying. Live-in Boyfriend
#1 couldn't handle that alone, so I covered the difference.

Months later, we started to regret our decision. We
always had enough to cover our monthly mortgage, but
we both had other debt that we weren't paying down.
Arguments over money followed. They added to the other
problems we were having. Seven months after we moved
in, Live-in Boyfriend #1, who had become my fiancé, took
a job with a newspaper in another city and moved out.

I was devastated. I had spent so much time with Live-in
Boyfriend #1 that I had forgotten what life was like before
him. To make matters worse, we couldn't have a clean
break because we owned property together. If it had not
been for that condo, our split would have been amicable.
Instead, we had to get lawyers involved.

About a year later, I met Live-in Boyfriend #2 when
Keith, the friend who later bought me the Knight in Shining
Armor, asked me to have drinks one night. I was on my
way home after a stressful day at work and refused his invitation at first because I was near my condo. But I changed
my mind and hailed a cab because I thought Keith would
cheer me up. Live-in Boyfriend #2, who was there with a
friend of Keith's, ended up being the one to cheer me up
that night. After Live-in Boyfriend #1 left, I was convinced
I could never fall in love again. But I did. Live-in Boyfriend
#2 and I declared our love for each other within a couple

of weeks, and I let him move in with me. It was a crazy decision but I was so in love that I wanted to spend all my free time with him.

Right before meeting Live-in Boyfriend #2, I had convinced the *Post* to let me report from our Baghdad bureau for two months. I had always wanted to be a foreign correspondent, and I particularly wanted to cover a war. Coincidentally, Live-in Boyfriend #2, also a journalist, was talking to another publication about going to Iraq. Fate seemed to be drawing us together. We would be in a war zone, dodging bullets by day and cuddling in our compound by night. It was a completely unrealistic view of a war zone, but we held on to it. Perhaps it was easier that way.

I left all my financial troubles behind when I went to Baghdad in November 2006. There's nothing better for your finances than living in a war zone. The *Post* had a house in a compound outside the fortified Green Zone, where the U.S. military and Iraqi parliament was headquartered. There were no bars, restaurants, shops for us. We had cooks. If we didn't eat at our house, we would go over to another news organization's bureau within the compound. All my expenses were covered, even the sweaters I needed when it got too cold. I never even touched money while I was there. I loved my two months in Baghdad, oddly enough, because I didn't have to worry about anything but work. No tossing and turning over the condo, over credit card bills, over my car payment.

When Live-in Boyfriend #2 and I left Baghdad, we were so exhausted and proud of ourselves that we splurged and hung out in Jordan, London, and Scotland for a couple of weeks. I finally had a healthier bank account thanks to two months of spending close to nothing. I had also gotten a friend of a friend to sublet my condo for half the mortgage. We hardly thought about money while we were traveling. We shopped, ate at nice restaurants, and drank. While eating sushi and drinking beer in London one afternoon, we looked at each other and declared life to be absolutely perfect.

Then we returned to DC, where life was not perfect. By that time, the real estate market was tanking. Ironically, my new beat at the *Post* was real estate. Every Sunday, I would look at the real estate ads—"Reduced by $50,000" and "Seller pays closing costs"—and break down in tears. "You know, you're going to have to figure out a way to deal with this if you're going to cover real estate," Live-in Boyfriend #2 said. "Otherwise, you're going to drive yourself crazy."

I did drive myself, and Live-in Boyfriend #2, crazy. But we still seemed very much in love when he was sent to Baghdad for another two-month tour. While he was gone, I managed to sell the condo, for $377,500, just $2,500 more than Live-in Boyfriend #1 and I had paid for it. We were lucky to sell it for that much because properties were depreciating rapidly. Even though we got more than we paid for it, we ended up losing most of the down payment because we had to pay the Realtors' commissions plus several other fees and taxes. Live-in Boyfriend #2 left me in charge of finding us a place to live while he was gone but suggested his old apartment building in Adams Morgan, a more eclectic and happening neighborhood. I found us a one-bedroom for $1,495.

I felt horrible about having to sell the condo and losing the down payment. Mostly, I felt bad about losing my mother's money. It would have hurt if it had been my own. But it hurt more knowing that it was the money that my mom had worked so hard to save. She insisted that the money was what she had tucked away for my inheritance. I would have gotten it anyway. She had also given my sister some money to help her buy a home. The only good thing to come out of dumping the condo was that I was finally free of Live-in Boyfriend #1, who at this point had also started dating someone else. For a year and a half I had had a financial connection to a man with whom I was not on speaking terms. Now I could finally move on with Live-in Boyfriend #2. He had what I call the five *S*'s. He was sweet, smart, successful, sexy, and single. We had survived a war zone together. We could survive anything.

Or so I thought.

A week before Live-in Boyfriend #2 was due back home, he told me he was going to spend a week embedded with the marines in one of the most dangerous parts of Iraq. As the week went by, I did not hear much from him, and I began to worry. I called his American cell phone and was surprised that it was ringing. That was my first clue that something was amiss. I left desperate messages. After making a few phone calls, I discovered he was not actually in Iraq. He had flown back to New York and had been there the entire week. I figured out what hotel he was at and called several times. No answer. I left messages. No callbacks. Desperate and confused, I got on a train and headed to New York. I arrived at 3:30 a.m. and rented a room in his hotel. A few hours later I managed to get his room number and knocked on his door. He opened it but tried to close it right away. It was too late. I could tell there was someone in his bed.

"Do you have someone with you?" I asked.

"Yes," he said.

I fled back to Washington, sobbing the whole train ride home. I got back to our apartment and packed his things. Friends came over to help me move his belongings to the basement. When he finally showed up hours later, two of my friends escorted him to the basement. I never saw him again.

I sunk into a deep depression after that. I couldn't eat, couldn't sleep. I decided to disappear for a week and a half. I had made Live-in Boyfriend #2 reimburse me for the cost of finding him in that hotel room. I took that money and my credit cards and hopped on a plane to California. I rented a white PT Cruiser convertible and drove up and down the Pacific Coast Highway, playing the Killers song, "When You Were Young" over and over again. (Opening line: "You sit there in your heartache/Waiting on some beautiful boy/To save you from your old ways.") I had friends to stay with at most of my stops. But at Pismo Beach, I rented a room by the ocean and had an expensive dinner alone at the restaurant. My biggest splurge was in San Diego. I had made no plans ahead of time. I just showed up and drove around until I saw a hotel that drew me to it. It was called the Ivy, and it had just opened. It had a great restaurant, a nightclub, and a rooftop bar that unbeknownst to me had become one of the city's most popular spots. I walked in and asked for a room. There was one available for about $400. I threw down my credit card. The room was small but spectacular. It had a spa-like shower, a big bed, a great view, and a well-stocked minibar. And here's the best part: I had my own butler. She arrived a few minutes after I checked in with a mini bottle of champagne and chocolate-covered strawberries.

"Are you here for business or pleasure?" she asked while opening the champagne.

"I just went through a divorce," I said. "I decided to treat myself to a vacation."

I felt like a divorced woman. I had gone through two terrible breakups in two years. I was exhausted, emotionally and physically. When I walked into that hotel, my eyes were puffy, my size 2 outfits were falling off me, and I could barely smile. I had not slept through the night in weeks. I kept waking up and replaying moments of our relationship and thinking, "What did I do wrong?" I would say things to myself like "I shouldn't have been grumpy that night the airline lost my bags in London. That's why he fell out of love with me, because I'm a bitch." When the butler left, I couldn't even bring myself to leave the room and see San Diego, which I had never visited before. I stayed in, ordered room service and a movie. The next day, I forced myself to the gym, then checked out and drove to the San Diego Zoo, where I burst into tears when I saw a camel. It reminded me too much of the Middle East.

Running Away

When I returned to DC, I threw myself into work, writing several front-page stories about the real estate market imploding. But I felt empty. Nothing was exciting me. I was also thinking a lot about my family and about how I had become so detached from them. I thumbed my nose at what I thought was their complacency in Queens. I was working on my career and traveling around the world while they were still eating Chinese food on Northern Boulevard. My sister called me a snob once, and she was completely right.

I had grown up speaking Spanish every day, eating rice and fried plantains, drinking the Colombian liquor aguardiente, and dancing to salsa and merengue tunes at my parents' parties. I now only spoke Spanish during my brief once-a-week phone calls to my parents, ate ahi tuna and avoided rice because low-carb diets were in, drank chardonnay, and went to parties where people stood around and talked about politics.

I started feeling that I had sacrificed my Hispanic self to become a yuppie. But then I thought, isn't this what my parents wanted? They wanted us to get good educations, to not be teased for mispronouncing words, to not be passed over for jobs because we were not American. They wanted us to be American. And we were, simply because they had made that journey to America and secured for us what they could never have for themselves—birth certificates showing we were born in New York City.

Like many Latino fathers his age, mine never talked much about himself. He was the head of the household, and we were to respect him at all times. He didn't reveal much about his life back in Colombia. But one weekend evening when we were all at home, my mother announced that my father's daughter from his first marriage would be visiting us. It was the first mention of her ever in our household. I think I was eight years old at the time. She was in her twenties. My dad had helped her make her way to America. Years later, I learned, through my older brother, Danny, who had somehow figured it out, that we also had a half brother in Colombia.

Fast-forward to September 2007. I was alone on a plane to Colombia to meet my half brother, Humberto. Call it part two of the Trejos Recovery Tour of 2007. I was reevaluating everything in my postbreakup depression, and decided I needed to reconnect with my roots. I wanted to see my dad's homeland, and I wanted to meet his other child. I thought somehow it would make me feel more Hispanic again and bring me closer to my family. Humberto was twenty years older than I am, but I found that he was just as lonely and heartbroken as I was. He lived alone in the hills near my dad's birth city of Pereira. His two daughters were living in Medellin. He was pining over a woman he had lived with for several years after his divorce. I spent four days with him in his sparsely furnished home, which had no hot water or cable TV. But it turned into a little sanctuary for me from the chaos I was living in back home. Humberto and I would spend hours walking around the city during the day and talking about our family at night. He was so sweet to me, even though in a sense, my mere existence was a reminder that he had grown up without a father.

I turned my visit into a *Washington Post* magazine piece, which paid for the trip and helped me sort though my emotions. But once again, every time I made a financial stride, I turned around and did something to put myself back in a financial rut. Still depressed and restless, I took a two-week, five-country tour of the Middle East with one of my best friends, Roy, in March 2008. I cannot say I regret that trip because I saw some of the most beautiful parts of the world (I highly recommend Baalbek, Lebanon). But I should have been paying off all my debt and saving money, not running around the world because I wanted to have fun and snap out of my depression.

Looking back at all my mishaps, I have realized a few things. Some people eat more when they're depressed. I spend more money. I am an impulsive shopper and traveler. Couple that with the emotional spending and you have a recipe for disaster. In my effort to understand why I have made these decisions, I contacted a few mental health professionals. After all, economics has always had a close link to psychology.

Personal Finance — It Is So Personal

Shortly after my trips to Colombia and the Middle East, I realized that I was living a hedonistic lifestyle in order to lessen the pain of my breakups. My life seemed so dreary that only the stimulation of shopping and traveling could make me feel better. My half brother was getting over his own heartbreak in a shack in the hills of Colombia, with no hot water. Me? I was buying pairs of jeans that cost more than some of my relatives down there paid in rent each month. Just like I had developed unhealthy relationships with men, I now had an unhealthy relationship with money. What was wrong with me?

"We have evolved into a culture that up until recently believed that money was the key to having everything we want and that everything we want is the key to happiness," said Laurie Nadel, a counselor with a private practice in Manhattan. "So then you realize that you have everything you want but you have all this debt and you can't manage it."

People in their twenties and thirties, in particular, have a strange relationship with money. That's because we have grown up with computers and access to hundreds of channels on our television sets. "The messages of advertising are designed around the myth, if you will, that when you buy something it will give you security, make you sexy, bring you social acceptance, make you feel better than the next person. It is based on what we want and not on what we need," she said.

Nadel and other counselors I talked to told me that being honest with my friends about my financial situation would help. How many times had I felt the pressure to go out to an expensive restaurant because all my friends were going? I was more willing to tell my friends how many people I have slept with than how much debt I was in.

We are unwilling to talk openly about our finances because in many of our families, money was either a taboo subject or a topic that sparked arguments. I don't remember my parents ever sitting any of us down when we were in high school and having an in-depth conversation about money. But why did I not study the way they handled money and emulate their frugal lifestyle? How did I develop such expensive tastes? I grew up in Queens with immigrant parents. How did I become this Sancerre-drinking, foie gras–eating crazy girl? In my effort to figure myself out, I asked Kathleen Burns Kingsbury, a licensed mental health counselor who is a money and emotions expert in Quincy, Massachusetts.

"Sometimes what we do is mirror what our parents do and sometimes we do the opposite," she said. "For people in their twenties and thirties and up, people getting out into the quote unquote real world, there's such pressure, if you're a girl, to have the right handbag, if you're a guy, to belong to the right golf club. There's incredible pressure to live above your means."

In other words, some people who grow up with frugal parents might feel deprived, and once they are calling their own shots, they buy the things they couldn't have as children.

So how do we craft a healthy relationship with money?

Mary Gresham, an Atlanta psychologist who specializes in money management, has an interesting theory. She said that people relate to money on three levels. On one level, it's a mathematical object. For instance, when you have a budget and you go to the grocery store and tell yourself you can only spend up to $100, you are treating money as a number. On another level, it's a carrier of symbols and emotions. When you break up with someone and buy yourself a Louis Vuitton purse, you are acting on emotions. On a third level, it's a symbol of what you value in your life. When you put aside money for your child's college education, you are showing that you value a college degree.

"People have a hard time thinking of these three levels separately, and they get mixed up. One minute they relate to it like it's a number, the next it's an emotion, and the next it's value. The sooner you can separate the three levels, and understand at which level you are operating, the sooner you'll become better with money," she said. "All three are important to do with skill. When people are trying to get ahold of their finances they try to do only the math level of money and not make any room for the other two. That's a mistake. And when you operate only emotionally, when you spend just because you feel like it at the moment, then you're making another kind of mistake."

I was definitely completely mixed up. But before I turned to sorting myself out, I had to deal with a major career change.

four
personal finance 101

When I returned from Iraq and my post–war zone journey through Europe in February 2007, I decided I needed a change at work. I had been a metro reporter for eight years, mostly covering schools. I had been roaming around the suburbs of Maryland looking for interesting stories for eight years. After two months in Baghdad, I was no longer interested in those stories. I looked around at the job openings at the paper and saw that the Financial section needed a real estate reporter. I applied, making the case that my struggle to sell my own condo would help me come up with good ideas for stories. I was right. For the next eight months, I wrote stories about people owing more for their houses than they could sell them for and about developers building way too many condos like mine.

In October 2007, an editor asked me if I would switch over to the personal finance beat.

"Are you kidding? I'm a personal finance disaster," I recall telling him.

As I contemplated the move, I worried that I was not qualified to write about what people should do with their money. Then I thought back to my pitch for the real estate job. Some of my best stories were born out of some experience I had. I wrote a story once about people dumping their real estate agents because I did the same thing when my agent was not able to sell my condo for the price we were asking. (The two agents I replaced her with sold it within a week; albeit for less money than she had tried to get me.)

I agreed to take the job. I started in November 2007. I decided I needed to teach myself the basics of personal finance. Neither my parents nor any of my teachers ever did, so it was up to me to learn. I talked to financial advisors. I read books. I read what other personal finance writers were writing.

I did not have a boyfriend at this point, so it was easy for me to throw myself into my work. If I could not excel in my love life, I needed to at least excel in my career. I could not have both parts of my life fall into shambles.

Your parents and teachers probably didn't teach you the basics of personal finance either. That's why so many of us are messes. So, I'm going to offer a few important tips I've learned on the job.

Living Within Your Means

I've obviously struggled with this concept. My friend Daphne, a journalist born and raised in France, has not. She has no credit card debt. Back home, she said, people take out loans for big-ticket items such as homes or cars. They don't take out loans for vacations and designer bags.

She doesn't understand why Americans think of the loans they get from credit card companies as free money.

Not only does Daphne not have credit card debt, but she also budgets. She knows what she earns each month. She knows what her fixed costs are. And she knows how much money she can spend each day on entertainment or dining or shopping. What a notion!

So the first step to becoming financially healthy is coming up with a budget. Too many people take out cash and don't pay attention to what happens to it. "They don't know what they spend," said Rolf M. Winch, a financial planner with Lifetime Financial Partners in Maryland. "If you don't know, how do you get your arms around it if you're in financial trouble?"

You can easily keep a budget with a personal finance program such as Quicken or Microsoft Money. Or you can do it on your own. Either way, you can take these steps:

1. *Calculate your monthly income.* How much do you have coming into your home from a regular job, a second job or freelancing gigs?
2. *Total up your monthly expenses.* List everything: rent, credit card bills, car payment, dry cleaning, utilities, toiletries, groceries, and anything else you spend your money on. Divide them up by fixed and variable expenses. Fixed expenses, such as rent, stay the same each month. Variable expenses, such as dining out, change. You may need to keep a diary for a few months to figure this out.

3. *Do the math.* Your monthly income minus your monthly expenses equals your discretionary cash flow.

4. *Adjust if necessary.* If you are spending more than you're taking in, cut out those variable expenses. Yes, that means getting a cheaper haircut each month or foregoing that weekend trip to New York. If you are spending less, put more toward savings. While writing this book at a coffeehouse one day, I spent $24 on a bagel with lox and two latte drinks. To compensate for that splurge the next day, I ate all my meals at home and didn't spend any money.

5. *Keep reevaluating your budget.* Even if you are within your budget, you should go through it each month and see if there are adjustments you need to make.

Score High

Readers constantly ask me if some action they are contemplating, such as opening a new credit card, is going to affect their credit score. Until I became a personal finance writer, I knew very little about credit scores, even though I should have. It's crucial for everyone to maintain a high credit score because lenders use this number to determine if they should give you a loan and at what interest rate. Your FICO credit score, which is the one that most lenders look at, ranges from 300 to 850. The higher your score, the lower your interest rate will be.

Your score is calculated based on information that the three credit reporting agencies—TransUnion, Experian, and Equifax—collect about you from your creditors. Your credit report will contain all your credit lines, public records such as bankruptcies and foreclosures, and any credit inquiries that have been made in the last two years. (A credit inquiry happens when you authorize a lender to pull your report. For instance, each time you apply for a credit card, your credit report will show it.)

You are legally entitled to get a free copy of your credit report once a year from each of the three agencies. You can request it at www.annualcreditreport.com or call 877-322-8228. Financial advisors recommend that you get a copy from each of the agencies at different points of the year so that you can see changes over time. Unfortunately, you have to pay to get your credit score. The best way to get your FICO score is to order it from myFico.com or through www.equifax.com. (TransUnion and Experian give consumers educational scores that they have developed and are typically not used by lenders.)

I went years without pulling my credit report. That was foolish. When I did finally do it, I noticed an error that probably damaged my score. I had to contact both the credit bureau and the creditor that provided the information. The credit bureau is required by law to correct any errors, but I had to wait almost three months to get it resolved.

It's important to know what factors affect your credit score. Here are some of them, which I found on myFico.com:

- Payment history, which shows if you've missed payments or have had any bankruptcies or any liens against you, counts for 35 percent.
- Amounts owed, which shows among other things the proportion of credit lines used (often referred to

as your credit utilization ratio, essentially telling you how maxed out you are), counts for 30 percent.

- Length of credit history counts for 15 percent. The longer you have a credit card, the better.
- New credit, which includes the number of recent credit inquiries, is 10 percent.
- Types of credit used, which shows the mix of accounts you have (i.e., mortgage, auto loan, credit cards), is the final 10 percent.

A few things that do not go into your credit score are your age, salary, and interest rates charged on your credit cards.

I made it a point to figure out how you can improve your score. Unfortunately, it takes time. Accurate negative information can stay in your credit report for up to seven years. But there are a few things you can do to keep your score high.

- Pay your bills on time. That's the most important thing. But if you've missed payments, catch up as soon as you can and stay current. The longer you pay your bills on time, the better your score.
- Keep your balances low on your credit cards. The proportion of credit lines used affects your score. In other words, the closer you are to being maxed out, the lower your score will be.
- Don't close unused credit cards. Many people do this thinking it will raise their score. It actually could

lower it because of the fact that the proportion of credit lines used affects your score.

- Don't open too many new cards at the same time. You might be tempted to do this to increase your available credit. But such a move could make you look like a risky borrower.
- If you are having trouble paying your credit cards, call your creditors and ask for a lower rate or other type of workout plan.

Debit or Credit: What's Your Flavor?

As I walked to the elevator with a coworker a few months after starting the personal finance beat, he asked if I was enjoying my new gig. I told him it was new territory for me but that I liked it so far. Then he told me that he has never had a credit card. I was shocked. Most people I know got their first credit card when they were in college. I admired him for not falling into the credit trap. But I also wondered what his credit history looked like.

The truth is, credit cards are a necessary evil. You need them to build a credit history. You also need them if you want to rent a car or if you have any kind of emergency.

But you don't have to rely on your credit card all the time. I like using my debit card because I know I am only spending money I have. Debit cards are linked to your bank account. That said, many banks enroll you in over-draft protection, which allows you to spend more than you have in your bank account—for a fee.

Also, debit cards do not always offer you as much

protection from identity theft as credit cards do. I learned this the hard way—twice! The first time I foolishly used my debit card to buy something in Africa and returned to find out that someone had gone on an online shopping spree for American Homie dolls. (They were gangster dolls. Apparently, they were in at one point.) The second time, I got a call from Bank of America notifying, me that someone was trying to buy hundreds of dollars' worth of running shoes out in Virginia. The manager at the store thought the woman was behaving oddly and called my bank. Unfortunately, the transaction had already gone through, but the woman had run out, realizing that the manager and cashier were suspicious. She didn't take off with the items, and the manager was more than willing to reverse the charge.

When that happened to me in January 2008, I decided to write a story about it. I learned that if someone fraudulently uses your credit card, you are reimbursed for nearly all the money lost. That may not be so with a debit card, especially if you do not notice it right away. Your liability is legally capped at $50 if you notify your bank in the first two business days. After that, you could lose up to $500. If you wait sixty days, you could lose it all. With credit cards, all you have to do is call your bank and dispute the charge. You usually get your money back right away.

Credit cards, when they are used responsibly, can actually be a big help. Let's say you need to pay a bill and you don't have the cash for it but you know you will have it in fifteen days. If you charge it, then pay off the bill before the interest starts racking up, that's not necessarily a bad thing.

Many cards also offer frequent-flier mile and cash-back

programs. However, you often have to pay an annual fee for the privilege. And if you don't pay off your card right away and carry a balance over to the next month, the interest you will pay on the charge will most certainly outweigh any of the benefits.

If you've decided to get a credit card, how do you go about finding a good one? There are many websites that compare cards, such as Bankrate.com, CardRatings.com, Credit.com, and CreditCards.com. Typically, if you think you're not going to pay off your card each month, you would want to go for a card with no annual fee and the lowest interest rate possible. If you know you're going to pay off your card each month, look for a card with the most lucrative rewards program possible and, preferably, no annual fee.

If You Don't Want to Stash Your Money Under a Mattress…

I remember how confused I was when I opened my first bank account in college. So I did the easiest thing: I went to the credit union on campus and got a basic checking account.

A credit union, which is formed by groups of people who have a common bond, such as the same employer or church, worked fine for me. But when I graduated I had to figure out where to take my money. This is not the easiest thing to do because there are so many options out there.

Aside from a credit union, you can also put your money in a bank or thrift. Over the years, the lines have blurred among these financial institutions, but there are some differences. Banks typically provide the widest variety of services, such as checking and savings accounts, certificates of deposit, mortgages, personal loans, and small business loans. Thrifts specialize in real estate lending but have expanded their services over the years. Credit unions tend to have better car loan rates and lower fees than banks and thrifts. Their credit cards also have an interest rate cap, which bank credit cards do not.

Given how so many financial institutions failed or merged in 2008 and 2009, you might want to know how protected your money is. The Federal Deposit Insurance Corporation (FDIC) insures deposits in banks and thrifts for up to $250,000 per depositor (that would be you). On January 1, 2014, the amount that is insured will decrease to $100,000, which is what it was before the financial crisis. Credit unions get the same protection through the National Credit Union Administration.

Once you decide on what type of financial institution to go for, you should think about what you want to accomplish. Do you want an account you can regularly tap into for transactions or do you want a place to park your money for a longer period of time?

A checking account is the best place to put your money if you need regular access to it. You can move money in and out of this account as often as you want through checks, ATM withdrawals, and electronic transfers. Some institutions will charge you a maintenance fee or require a minimum balance, but you really don't have to put up with that. There are plenty of reputable institutions with no such requirements.

A savings account also allows you to make deposits and withdrawals, but you are usually limited in the number of withdrawals you can make. You also usually cannot write checks from this account, but you can make ATM withdrawals.

Many checking and savings accounts will pay you interest, but often not enough to beat the rate of inflation, which means that in a few years, your money won't get you as far. Many online banks, such as ING Direct, sometimes offer accounts with higher rates. Websites such as Bankrate.com compare the rates offered by various financial institutions.

A money market account pays more interest than a checking or savings account. But there is often a minimum balance required to start earning that interest. And withdrawals are limited to six per month.

The other option you will come across is the certificate of deposit (CD). You agree to leave your money in the account for a certain amount of time. In exchange, you earn more interest than you do with the other accounts. Greg McBride, senior financial analyst for Bankrate.com, recommends this option only if you already have a checking account and a savings vehicle that you can access for emergencies. "This is money that you're willing to part with for a while," he said.

Saving Versus Investing

If you have any money left over after you pay all your bills, what should you do with it?

Don't park it all in a savings account, but don't put it all in the stock market either. Set aside at least six months' worth of living expenses in emergency cash reserves.

Beyond that, you should invest some money to meet your long-term financial goals. This is the only way your money is going to grow. But let's face it: If you're in your twenties and thirties, you're not going to have all that much extra money to play around with in the stock market. At the very least, you need to invest your money through a 401(k) or an Individual Retirement Account (IRA). A 401(k) is a retirement savings account offered by employers that allows you to invest your money before it is taxed. There are several types of IRAs, all of which offer some sort of tax break. There are many ways you can invest the money you save in these accounts. Most people put them in mutual funds, which are run by professional managers who decide what stocks, bonds or other vehicles to buy. I will describe in Chapter 13 some of your other investment options.

Dealing with Uncle Sam

It's probably the most dreaded day of the year: April 15, the day you have to file your taxes. This is how the federal and state governments (or city in my case) determine if they've taken too much money or not enough out of your paycheck. When you start your job, your employer will ask you to fill out an Internal Revenue Service form called a W-4. This will determine how much money is withheld from each paycheck. The amount you have withheld will depend on factors such as your marital status and how many children or dependents you have. On this form, you have to state how many exemptions you want to claim on your taxes. Each exemption is worth a certain amount of money, which changes each year. The more exemptions you request, the more money you will take home each pay period. The fewer you request, the less money you will take home. You can adjust your withholdings any time you feel you need to. The IRS website, www.irs.gov, has a withholding calculator you can use to figure it out.

Now how should you go about filing your taxes each year? There are so many forms on the IRS website, but the main one you have to worry about is the 1040. There are different variations of it. The 1040 is the long form, which you use if you're going to itemize your deductions (that is, try to write off some of your expenses for the year). If you don't have a complicated tax situation, then you can use the simpler 1040A, aka the short form, or the even simpler 1040EZ, aka the easy form.

You will have to decide if you're going to do your taxes on your own or if you're going to pay someone to do them. If you have friends who are good at doing their taxes and are willing to do yours, even better. This is really a matter of personal preference. If your situation is simple enough to warrant use of the short or the easy form, you probably don't need to spend what could end up being a few hundred dollars on a professional. I used to do my own taxes but hired an accountant when my finances got more complicated.

Either way, you're going to have to be a good record keeper. Expect to start receiving all your tax documents in January. Your employer will send your W-2 form, which details your wages and taxes withheld. You will get forms from your student loan company, your bank (if you earned interest on any of your accounts), the firm that handles your investments if you have any, etc. Also collect any receipts for donating furniture or clothing or making contributions to a charity or church. And if you are a freelancer or have other employment aside from your regular job, keep receipts for all your expenses. Those could be tax deductible.

What do you do if you owe money and don't have it? Many tax lawyers and accountants I've talked to said a lot of people simply don't file their taxes. "If you don't file, a number of things can happen, and all of them are bad," said Burton J. Haynes, a tax attorney in Burke, Virginia.

You incur penalties for not filing a return, anywhere from 5 percent per month of lateness to 25 percent of the amount due. The IRS can also determine your tax liability on its own in what is called a "substitute for return." You certainly don't want that to happen because the agency usually comes up with a number that is much higher than what you owe. Even worse, you can actually be prosecuted for willful failure to file.

If you do file a return and have a tax liability, financial planners and other experts said you should do what you can to cobble together the money. That means raiding your bank accounts and sofa cushions, cashing in those IOUs, and yes, perhaps begging your relatives for loans.

If none of these options works, you should offer the IRS a portion of what you owe, then ask if you can pay the rest in installments.

Finally, you can try to get the IRS to accept what is known as an "offer in compromise," under which the agency agrees to take less than what it is owed. That can take a lot of time and effort.

Thankfully, I had not gotten into any trouble with the IRS, but I had other issues to deal with. That's why I decided to get some professional help.

five
take my hand

Finding a good financial planner is like finding a good therapist. I have yet to find a therapist I haven't dumped after five sessions. I was determined to do a better job with my financial planner. It's easier to talk about all my failed relationships and my neurosis about my weight than it is to talk about how I have utterly mismanaged my finances. Smart people can sometimes make bad choices in mates, but they're supposed to know that carrying a credit card balance is, well, not smart. Here I was not only about to admit to this person that I had screwed up—and badly at that—but I was also about to hand over all of my bank, credit card, and 401(k) statements to prove it. I had to make sure he or she was worthy of it.

"You're trusting somebody with everything you've worked for your whole life. That's a really big responsibility," said Linda Dalby, a partner at the Boston law firm Day Pitney, who advises clients on how to handle their money.

I didn't have to hire a financial planner to fix my finances. I could have gone to a credit counselor instead who might have been able to negotiate payment plans with all my creditors. Or I could have just done my own research, which I do all the time for my job, and fixed myself on my own. But I interview enough financial planners to make me wonder why so many people seek professional help when it comes to money. Some people would rather drink lots of water and take vitamin C when they've got a cough. I tend to be the going-to-the-doctor type. So I figured, why not apply this to my finances?

It was late summer 2008, and the economy was getting worse. More and more people were falling behind on their mortgages, car loans, and credit card payments. The stock market was crashing. Banks were failing. Gas prices were skyrocketing. Companies were laying off people. And it all started years before when some bankers came up with the idea to give people mortgages with interest rates that would remain the same for only two or three years rather than the traditional thirty.

Each day I would interview people who were in trouble and experts who were trying to help them out of trouble. I couldn't keep it up. So I started doing research on finding a planner. If you too decide to go the planner route, here are the steps to take.

- *Decide on your financial objectives.* What kind of advice do you want? Do you want to get out of debt? Start on your retirement planning? Buy a life insurance policy? Or all of the above? Different planners have different specialties.
- *Shop around.* There are plenty of financial planners out there. To find a legitimate one in your area, try these organizations: the Financial Planning Association

(www.fpanet.org), the National Association of Personal Financial Advisors (www.napfa.org), the American Institute of Certified Public Accountants (www.aicpa .org), and the Society of Financial Service Professionals (www.financialpro.org). You can also ask your friends and colleagues for recommendations, but beware, said Barry Glassman, a financial advisor and senior vice president at Cassaday and Company in McLean. "When friends recommend their advisors, we have to keep in mind that part of that referral is that they want to justify their own decision." Plus, he said, "We're friends with our friends but we have to understand what their personality is with money. It may be different than ours."

- *Check their credentials.* There are many people out there who say they are qualified to give financial advice. Guess what? They're not all qualified. Check with the Certified Financial Planner Board of Standards, Inc. (www.cfp.net/search) and other professional organizations. Find out how long they have been in practice. Ask them to describe their work history and give you references.
- *Check their disciplinary history.* Yes, some planners have been disciplined for doing such things as selling grandmothers bad insurance policies. So make sure your planner has a clean record. Aside from the CFP board, you can also check with the Securities and Exchange Commission (www.sec.gov), the North

American Securities Administrators Association (www
.nasaa.org), and the Financial Industry Regulatory
Authority (www.finra.org).

- *Figure out how they expect to be compensated.* There
are many ways planners get paid. Some receive
salaries from their companies. Some receive commissions for products they sell their clients, such as
life insurance policies, by the companies that make
those products. And some charge a fee based on a
flat rate or a percentage of their clients' assets. This is
very important because you don't want your planner
to have any conflicts of interest. "The people who
work for companies that sell products are paid by
commission for the product they sell and therefore
don't have your best interest in mind," said Dalby.
"There are fee-based planners who just charge you
by the hour or have a fixed rate. They can be better but it doesn't guarantee the quality of what they
say. It just means they don't have that conflict of
interest."
- *Interview them.* It's important to get along with your
planner. Meet up with him or her to see if you click.
Also, take the time to figure out how he or she
works. Some questions to ask are: How often do you
expect to meet? Do you prefer talking by phone or in
person? What is your approach to financial planning?
How many other clients do you have? Do you have
experience working with young people?
- *Get your agreement in writing.*

What Assets?

I started my search in August 2008 by e-mailing Rita Cheng, a certified financial planner in Bethesda whom I had interviewed for stories several times. I liked Rita. She was smart and engaging. But I figured I had worked with her too often in my role as a reporter to hire her as my planner. I told her I wanted a planner who was tough but compassionate. Someone who would help me come up with a budget and follow it. I also wanted someone who would charge a flat fee. I wanted to make sure my planner would work toward putting more money in my wallet, not in his or hers. She sent me a few names and e-mails. Christine Parker, a certified financial planner based in Maryland, seemed like a promising candidate. She was president of Parker Financial, an independent fee-only advisory firm. I liked what she had to say on her website: "Our mission is to help clients plan well to live well."

I chose a Starbucks two blocks from my office in downtown DC as the venue for our first meeting. Perhaps I was trying to make a statement. Even in my effort to fix my finances, I was not going to completely give up the occasional latte or caramel macchiato.

As usual, I was running late that morning. So instead of the bus, I took an $8 taxi. What a way to start my journey toward financial stability. Bad Nancy, I mumbled to myself, as I handed the money to the driver.

I walked in and looked around. Even though I had never seen a picture of her, I could spot her immediately. She had short brown hair, glasses, seemed to be in her forties, and wore a skirt and matching blazer. She was patiently sipping her drink at a table near the bathroom with a stack of papers in front of her. I darted toward her. "Hi, I'm Nancy. I'm so sorry I'm late,"

"That's okay," she said with a big smile. What a warm smile, I thought. I liked her already.

We shook hands, then I excused myself because I desperately needed caffeine. I ordered a regular coffee, worried that buying a more expensive latte would make her think I was not serious about this. I did, however, buy a bottle of water because I just couldn't bring myself to drink the lead-laden DC tap water.

I sat down and told her what my goal was: To get—and stay—out of debt.

"I have it all," I said. "Credit card debt, a car loan, student loan debt."

She nodded and smiled as she listened. Then she told me about herself. She does a lot of pro bono work, she said, because she was raised by a single mother who struggled with money.

Yay, I thought. She has empathy. I love people with empathy.

"I know how hard this can be," she said. "You live in an expensive city, and you want to live a certain lifestyle. I can try to help you figure out how to do that."

It was exactly what I wanted to hear. I don't subscribe to the philosophy that you have to live a completely ascetic lifestyle in order to be financially responsible. I am young and single and I want to have some fun. I know fun can be expensive, but I truly believe there is a way to budget so that you can splurge every once in a while. I just had not yet figured out how to do that.

She handed me a big black leather case. It was quite nice. I get so excited when I score free things. Then she told me what it was for. She asked me to fill it with all my credit card, student loan, car loan, and bank statements, plus a pay stub and any other document that would help her determine what my net worth was. Suddenly the nice leather case seemed so ominous.

"My net worth?" I asked, my forehead wrinkling up. "What if my net worth is negative?"

"I've worked with people with negative net worth," she said.

That made me feel only slightly better. Can you imagine being told that you're worth nothing? Am I worth nothing?

We decided to meet again once I had a chance to gather all of my papers.

Shortly after, I had coffee with my friend and coworker Deborah. She has been in debt before so I often whine to her about my financial problems. I told her about having to turn to my parents for help. "I am in my thirties. Why can't I figure out how to get it right?" I asked, my arms waving around all over the place as they often do when I am upset or nervous.

"I have no assets," I said, as we sat in the *Post*'s cafeteria. I buried my head in my hands. It wasn't technically true, for I did have a 401(k) retirement account and a car, but I still felt like I had nothing.

Deborah laughed. "You may have no assets, but you have smarts," she said.

It was my turn to laugh, so loudly that others in the cafeteria turned to look.

She was right. What I lack in assets, I make up for in smarts, and it was time for me to start using them.

Unfortunately, the country's financial crisis only worsened after my first meeting with Christine, which meant I was suddenly busier than usual at work. Our next meeting didn't come until more than a month later.

We picked the same Starbucks. But first, I had to gather all the papers she had requested. That in itself sent me into a tizzy.

I keep all of my financial documents in a file cabinet next to my desk at home. I have them divided into file folders with labels such as "Bank Statements—Citibank," "Car Loan," "Social Security," "Trip receipts." They are alphabetized and stuffed with statements dating back to the late 1990s. I deposit all my documents in there and forget about them, only returning to them when I get a third bill from a doctor for an unpaid balance in the hopes of being able to prove him or her wrong. I always think, Wait, I already paid that bill. I can prove it. Then I run to the file cabinet and realize that I can't.

The night before our meeting, I pulled out everything she asked for, then went online to get copies of statements that I now only get electronically. I smoked many cigarettes as I did this. (Yes, I must quit that habit, if not for my health, then for my wallet. They cost $7.50 a pack.)

I sat down to fill out an eighteen-page questionnaire she had e-mailed me.

First, there was the perfunctory information: age, employment, etc.

Then came the hard part.

Age to retire? I jotted down 65, knowing full well after getting my last 401(k) statement, which was about $3,000 less than the previous statement because I owned too many shares of my own company's stock, that 65 was probably too ambitious.

Under "Financial Goals—Major Purchases, Weddings, Travel, New Home, etc.," there was room for three. These were mine:

1. To be debt-free.
2. To be able to travel occasionally.
3. To be able to go out a few nights a week.

I skipped over the "Philanthropy and Planned Giving" section. Someday, I thought. Not now.

Then came the really painful part—listing my assets. My two bank accounts were pathetic-looking. I had just over $2,000 total. My 401(k) had just under $32,000.

I had more to list under liabilities: $12,960 on my Citibank credit card, $2,231 on my U.S. Airways MasterCard, $11,500 for my Sallie Mae student loan, and $10,670 for my HSBC car loan.

I had a couple more cigarettes, brushed my teeth, washed my face, then got into my bed and pulled my duvet over my head. I just wanted to fall asleep and not deal with anything.

The next morning, I again was running late. Another taxi. Another Bad Nancy mutter to the sky as I paid the driver.

Again, Christine was waiting patiently, this time with a laptop. This time, she offered to buy me a drink. I took advantage of this and ordered a skim latte, but I made it a tall one rather than a grande.

We chitchatted. She said she had been reading my stories and was very impressed.

Wait until she sees my financial records, I thought. Not impressive.

"Okay, what have you got for me?" she asked.

We looked at my goals.

"To be debt-free."

It was at this point that Christine made me realize something important. Few people are debt-free. Most people have someone they owe money to, whether it's a student loan company or a dentist or a mortgage company. And frankly, a cursory review of my assets and liabilities at that point showed that it was impossible for me to be debt-free anytime soon. We all need to set realistic goals when it comes to our finances.

"You want to be in a position where you feel the debt is manageable," she offered as a revision to Goal Number 1.

I agreed and rewrote it: "To be able to manage my debt by the end of 2008."

We then had to look at my life expectancy because even though I was only concerned with the immediate, Christine told me I had to keep in mind what I'm going to need to be financially stable for the rest of my life, not just now. People are living longer and must plan to have enough to get them through age ninety. She looked at my parents' ages. I told her that my paternal grandfather lived until almost a hundred.

"For you, I think we need to plan for ninety-nine," she said.

I suddenly started thinking of a story that my editor had forwarded me from the *Onion*. It described a scene between a financial planner and his client. The client's stock portfolio had been decimated by the huge drops in the Dow Jones Industrial Average. The planner turned to the client and recommended that he die at an earlier age because there was no way he would have enough to get him through retirement.

Okay, the fact that I was thinking so much about death was starting to scare me. You want to live, Nancy. You want to live, I told myself.

And travel. "How many times a year do you want to travel?" Christine asked.

I wanted to travel every month. Traveling is perhaps my favorite thing to do. It's the reason I became a journalist. I remember getting sucked into TV news and newspapers during the first Persian Gulf War, when I was a sophomore in high school, and thinking: That's what I want to do with my life. I want to go overseas and tell people back home what's going on.

By the time I got to college, I had left the country only once, to visit relatives in Colombia. My first big overseas trip after I graduated was to Paris. I met up with my friend Emily Wax there. She was the *Post*'s correspondent in Nairobi at the time. We spent five days together in Paris, drinking great wine, eating fantastic salads and cheese, buying jewelry and trench coats, gazing at beautiful works of art, and posing for photos everywhere we could. Once she returned to Africa, I spontaneously took the train to London to visit my former college roommates.

I started exploring pretty regularly after that. The following year, I went to Nairobi to visit Emily. We went to Rwanda to cover the tenth anniversary of the genocide. We drove through the mountains from Kigali to a town near the Democratic Republic of Congo. Then we returned to Kenya for a safari.

I fell in love with the Middle East after my two months in Baghdad, so I kept going back to the region. I've been to Beirut four times.

I am digressing. The point is, I love traveling and I tend to spend money on it without thinking about the consequences.

Back to the question at hand. How many times a year did I want to travel, or how many times a year could I travel?

"Once?" I asked sheepishly.

"That's fine," Christine said. She was jotting down notes. "We are going to budget for one trip a year. That way you can travel, without the guilt associated with it."

Next, we looked at my desire to go out every once in a while. "How much do you want to spend on going out?"

The truth is, I spend a lot on meals and booze with my friends. After my horrible breakup with Live-in Boyfriend #2, I started going out almost every night to avoid moping at home.

"Well, I'd like to go out three times a week," I said.

She suggested $100 a week, which in DC doesn't go very far. Just two nights before, my friend Amit, who had just returned from a one-year stint in our Baghdad bureau, didn't have to try very hard to convince me to go out to dinner. We each had an appetizer and an entrée and split a bottle of wine. It cost us $70 each. But I persuaded myself I could get by with $100 a week.

"Let's talk about your long-term goals," Christine said.

I thought we had been already. She wanted to talk about retirement again? "How can I think about retirement when I can't deal with life now?"

She said she understood that but that I needed to think about making myself financially healthy for the long term. That meant putting as much as I could away in my 401(k). That meant having my health, disability, and life insurance in order. That meant having a living will. And that meant having at least six months' worth of living expenses in an emergency cash reserves fund.

"That's why people fall into bankruptcy," she said. "If they had that money set aside, they would still be able to pay their bills."

We decided that one of my goals would be to save for emergencies.

At this point, Christine asked me about my family.

"We learn about money from our families," she said.

"The stresses it causes. The values our parents have. Did they instill in you being thrifty?"

I gave her a short summary about my parents' frugal habits. Their love of KFC. Their disdain for shopping. Their desire to save, save, save.

"I don't know what went wrong with me," I said. "I think I just rebelled. I think I just didn't want to have that lifestyle. I wanted a different lifestyle."

"It's difficult for young people to live that lifestyle in a city," Christine said.

We moved on. "If you had to put a value on what you own what would that be?"

I laughed. I owned lots of dresses, lots of shoes, some furniture, a bit of gold jewelry, tons of books and DVDs, some CDs, many battered cell phones, a very slow laptop, a camera, and lots of tchotchkes, as Emily likes to call knick-knacks. Oh, and a car that I really didn't own because I owed the bank more than ten grand for it. And the Knight in Shining Armor.

"Well that's something," she said. "Would you say $5,000? $10,000?"

"Let's say $5,000."

She was making me jot down a list of Action Items. So far I had "Sign living will." She made me jot down "Take photos of belongings for insurance purposes."

I had brought with me my Open Enrollment form for all my employee benefits. It was that time of year.

She looked at my life insurance and determined that I had too much. Before I went to Iraq, I had upped my life insurance to much more than the standard one year's salary. I even got extra dismemberment insurance. I figured that would be a good thing to have in the land of IEDs. Christine thought I only needed one year's worth of life insurance and way less dismemberment insurance.

"If something happened to you, you have no one to take care of," she pointed out. "This would be enough to cover your debt. The rest would go to your beneficiary."

Ouch. What a way to remind me that I am all alone. No husband, no children, no pets.

We were an hour into our session and we had not even looked at my debt. It turned out we weren't going to do that during this meeting. I handed her all of my documents. The next step would be for her to crunch numbers and come up with a budget. We decided to meet the following Monday morning. Same time, same place.

"Is this going to work?" I asked her as we gathered our belongings.

"It's got to work," she said. "You have no other choice."

Day of Reckoning

I was dreading Monday. I knew life as I knew it would be over after that day. I would have to get serious and get my life in order. My year of rampage, as my friend Eric calls it, which by this point was really a year and a half of rampage, would have to end.

I took the bus to the Starbucks this time. I was fifteen minutes late but proud of myself for taking the frugal option.

Christine had my budget ready.

First, we looked at my credit card debt.

The average credit card interest rate that week, she told me, was between 11.04 and 13.82 percent.

Of my two credit cards, she wanted me to pay off the one with the lowest balance first.

"Shouldn't I try to pay off the one I owe more to?" I asked.

No, she explained, because that one had the lowest rate—10.99.

My U.S. Airways MasterCard had a 15.24 percent rate. "If you keep that balance, you pay more interest over time," she said.

Now, I get frequent-flier miles for using that. "You have to weigh if the miles you get are worth the interest you're paying on that balance," she said.

That became the next Action Item.

"Try to live within the income you take home," she said.

My annual salary was $86,000 a year before taxes. It has not budged much the last couple of years because the newspaper industry has not been doing so well. I realize that $86,000 is more than what most Americans make, but in a city as expensive as DC, it doesn't go as far as it would in other parts of the country. I was taking home about $3,960 a month, $1,500 of which goes toward housing.

"Basically, try to live within your means," she said.

I've been hearing that phrase a lot lately.

"We need to work on increasing your net worth," she said.

Now, she was about to tell me exactly what my net worth is. I braced myself.

$2,265.

"I have net worth!" I exclaimed in glee.

"Yes, you do," she said with a smile.

While I was obviously not going to be debt-free by the end of 2008, I could have my debt under control by then, she said.

Then, we were going to work on having me reserve $8,800 to $17,000 in my emergency fund. "That's not going to happen by the end of the year, but that is something you can work on," she said.

She asked me to put $50 to $100 in a savings account once a month. "I know that's hard to think about when you're trying to make ends meet, but let's get through November and see where we are," she said. I had already canceled my cable, which would save me a little more than $100 a month. I would have to stash that in a savings account.

I wasn't overspending on rent, she said, which was good. I was overspending on fun, which was bad.

She gave me what I thought was a healthy monthly allowance for food and entertainment: $300 for food and $400 for entertainment and dining. She even said I could set aside $250 a month for recreation and travel. Another $200 would go toward personal care items and $75 toward dry cleaning. Beyond that, I had $125 for my phone and $50 for utilities.

My debts would be paid off as follows each month: $150 to the U.S. Airways card, $254 to the Citibank, $297 to my car, $99 to Sallie Mae.

I would have $260 in discretionary income. "Tight, very tight," she said.

There was no allowance for shopping for clothing.

Okay, I thought, I had enough pretty scarves and shoes to make each outfit I have look a little bit different. I could get away with it.

There was silence as I contemplated this. "If you feel it's too much at one time, then take it in steps," she said.

More silence. I just wanted to listen to all her reassurances. She said I was not in terrible shape.

"You're at the cusp. That's key. I'd like to see you with more cash at hand. All that is, is living within your means, within a budget each month. That's where everyone gets into trouble. It's not the rent. It's all the other things they're doing. It doesn't mean you have to sit at home every night alone and bored. But we have to get you living within your means."

Live within your means. Live within your means.

I suddenly thought of a line in one of Woody Allen's films. My friend Daphne had told me she had recently heard it and thought of me. It is morbid but seemed appropriate at the time. "Death should not be seen as the end, but as a very effective way to cut down on expenses."

six
the kiss of debt

My planner Christine said I should take my quest for financial security one step at a time. I agreed and came up with a number of financial problems and issues, from the serious to the not so serious, with which I was struggling. Yes, I had to learn how to save better for retirement and pay off my car and student loans. But it was also important for me to become a more responsible consumer of clothing and cosmetics, for instance, because I do happen to live in a capitalist society.

My biggest liability, however, was my credit card debt. It was clear to me that I had to tackle that first.

When I met with Christine in fall 2008, I had five credit cards. One was a Citibank with a balance of about $12,960 and a 10.99 percent interest rate. My U.S. Airways Master-Card, for which I get frequent-flier miles, had a balance of about $2,231 and a 15.24 percent interest rate. I also had Neiman Marcus and Ann Taylor cards, which I owed nothing on. I can't even tell you what that $15,000 or so bought me. I believe the bulk of it went to dresses, shoes, Broadway plays, concerts, trips, and dinners. Was it worth it? I've had a lot of fun over the years, but being in debt is no fun at all.

Each month, I was sending Citibank $300, which was more than the minimum payment. I was sending U.S. Airways about $80, which was also more than the minimum required. This wasn't the wisest financial move, Christine told me. I should be sending more to the credit card with the highest interest rate.

Christine suggested I call U.S. Airways MasterCard to ask them to lower my rate. I should tell them that if they didn't, I would transfer my balance to my Citibank card because it has a lower rate. "It might be tough with the credit crunch, but you have nothing to lose by trying," she said.

It was tough. Actually, it was impossible. I had owned the card for less than a year. The customer service representative on the other side of the line told me I had not yet established enough of a payment history with them and therefore could not qualify for an interest rate deduction.

So what were my other options?

I could continue to whittle down the debt, but Christine said I would have to send less to Citibank and more to U.S. Airways each month.

I could transfer my U.S. Airways card balance to my Citibank card. Citibank sent me a few balance transfer checks that would give me a 0.99 percent interest rate until December 2009. But I would have to pay a fee of 3 percent of the transferred balance. Something I had to keep in mind was how such a move would affect my credit score. If I got too close to maxing out one card, I could end up with a lower score. In fact, Christine said, it's usually not a good idea to use more than 50 percent of the available credit on any one card.

My Citibank card had a $25,000 limit. Transferring my U.S. Airways balance to my Citibank card would get me over that 50 percent mark and make it difficult to get more credit at a decent rate. But it might be a trade-off worth making, Christine said.

Christine ran some numbers for me. If I kept my U.S. Airways card at 15.24 percent and sent in $40, or the minimum, each month, it would take me 98 months to pay it all off. In that time, I would have paid about $1,689 in interest.

My Citibank balance at the 10.99 percent interest would take me 56 months to pay off if I sent in $300 a month. In the end, I would have paid about $3,840 in interest.

Now, if I moved my U.S. Airways balance to my Citibank card, I would have to pay the 3 percent balance transfer fee. That translated to about $67. Add that to the U.S. Airways balance, and I would owe Citibank an extra $2,300 or so. At the bank's 0.99 percent rate, I could still wipe it out more quickly.

"The positive is you're getting away from the 15.24 percentage. You're getting a good introductory rate and you're combining your debt. It's easier to make a bigger payment in one lump sum," Christine said. "The negative is you're increasing the balance on one card, which might affect your FICO score. And if you clear the balance on the U.S. Airways card, you have to get rid of the temptation to use it again. But you don't want to close it because it helps your FICO score. I would put it in a Baggie and put it away."

If I didn't want to go that route, I could try to get a credit union or my bank to give me a personal loan so that I could consolidate my debt at a lower interest rate. But by the time I was trying to do this toward the end of 2008, all financial institutions had become squeamish about lending money to anyone. Banks were losing money and they didn't want to lose any more by lending to people with a lot of debt.

Finally, I could tap into my 401(k) retirement savings plan through a hardship withdrawal that would then be taxed as income by the IRS. Planners don't like that option because it severely drains your retirement accounts. You lose out on that savings compounding, which ultimately shrinks your nest egg.

I e-mailed Christine to get her take on the 401(k) bailout option. Not surprisingly, she called it the "last resort," only to be done if you cannot make your monthly debt payments or are at risk of default, foreclosure, or bankruptcy. I was not in any of those situations.

For my purposes, she pointed out another big danger: "Unfortunately, when debt is paid off in a lump sum and spending habits have not changed, credit card debt can increase and you're right back in the same position," she said.

She urged me to stick with my monthly spending and savings plan. I heeded her advice and decided to leave my 401(k) alone. Instead, I went for the balance transfer option.

Consolidating my debt gave me a small sense of relief. I was taking steps to rid myself of my debt. But I knew full well that even if I cut back on spending, stopped using my credit cards, and stuck to a budget, it would still take me a long time to be debt-free. This was a sobering realization.

Tricks of the Trade

Ironically, my job was requiring me to become a credit card expert. I almost wished I had become a personal finance writer sooner. A bit of historical perspective and an understanding of how credit card issuers do business could have made me a smarter borrower. But here I was writing story after story about how America's problem with credit cards helped lead us into a recession just as I was trying to sort out how to handle my own debt.

I set out to find out how credit cards became such a big part of the American economy. Legend has it that financier Frank X. McNamara and some colleagues came up with the idea for the first charge card because they forgot to take enough cash with them to pay for their New York City power lunch one day in 1949. Soon after that, they launched a network of restaurant charge accounts known as the Diners Club. Its intended target: Rich businessmen and jetsetters who wanted an easy way to pay for expensive meals.

In September 1958, Bank of America mailed 60,000 all-purpose charge cards, named BankAmericards, to almost every household in Fresno, California.

The Fresno Drop, as it was called, helped usher in an era of easy credit for the average American. Before then, Americans paid for almost everything in cash, either at the time of purchase or through an installment plan with an individual merchant. The only credit they could get was through a loan with a bank, which required them to physically appear before a loan officer and plead for money.

The experiment was a disaster at first. The bank had

not set up proper collections or fraud departments. The delinquency rate reached 22 percent.

For some reason, Bank of America's executives, perhaps unwilling to admit their mistake, chose not to give up on the experiment even though they had lost millions of dollars. Their perseverance paid off. From 1960 to 1968, the number of cards in use almost doubled to more than 400,000. In 1960, there was $59 million worth of sales. In 1968, the company made $400 million off the cards, according to Joseph Nocera, who described the Fresno Drop in his 1994 book *A Piece of the Action: How the Middle Class Joined the Money Class.*

Clearly, it didn't take long for Americans to become addicted to debt. In 1968, total credit card debt was $8 billion in current dollars. Americans now carry around $900 billion worth of credit card debt. The average borrower has a $5,710 credit card balance, according to TransUnion, one of three companies that produce the credit reports. Other reputable sources estimate the average balance is closer to $10,000, which makes me feel a little better since my own part of the credit pile surpassed $10,000.

At the end of 2008, we were told we were officially in a recession. In fact, we had technically been in one since December 2007. At the beginning of 2009 came more sobering news: According to the Fitch Ratings Credit Card Index, payments made at least sixty days late increased to a record high of 3.75 percent. Many Americans were in trouble.

And it dawned on me that I was, too. I had had a long stretch of paying my credit card bills on time, but by the middle of 2008 I was realizing that the payments I was sending in weren't making much of a dent.

Why was this? The answer is not as simple as: My balance is just too high. Even borrowers who always pay on time can get hit with rising interest rates and hidden fees. That's because the industry came up with so many ways to keep borrowers tethered to their cards. They were able to do these things freely up until 2010.

Have you ever heard of universal default? Say you've never been late sending your monthly payment to Card Company #1, but you've missed a payment or two to Card Company #2. Every so often, Card Company #1 will look at your credit report. If it sees what you've done to Card Company #2, guess what? Card Company #1 could increase your rate.

I also learned that card companies allocate payments in a way that makes it harder for borrowers to pay off their debt. It's quite common to have two or more interest rates on the same card. For instance, you might have received a cash advance. That balance will typically carry a higher interest rate than the amount you owe on your purchases. This is how your card company will usually deal with it: Each month, it will apply your payment to the balance with the lowest rate. That way the balance with the higher rate will keep accumulating and compounding interest, squeezing more money out of your pocket.

They also don't give you much time to send in a payment. Often, they'll send you your monthly statement fourteen days before your payment is due. Keeping track of your due date each month isn't always easy. That's because credit cards can change your due date without much notice or specify a particular time of the day when it is due. If you're an hour late, you're screwed. You'll get hit with a late fee, usually along the lines of $15 to $39. Or worse, your interest rate could go up substantially.

And then there's the most bizarre practice of all: Double-cycle billing. Credit card companies often reach back to the previous billing cycle when calculating the interest rate charge for the current cycle's balance. Okay, you're probably scratching your head right now. I sure scratched mine when I first heard of this. Companies compute finance charges on your average daily balance by adding each day's balance then dividing it by the total number of days in the billing cycle. Many use the average daily balance over the last two billing periods. So if you have a balance one month and pay a finance charge on it, you will also end up paying a finance charge for the next month even if you've paid off the balance by that time.

Travis Plunkett, legislative director for the Consumer Federation of America, called such practices destabilizing to families, especially during a recession. "The credit card industry has been able to do whatever they want. The days of offering families unsustainable loans that help push them over the financial brink is gone, and we have to acknowledge that all credit is not good credit," he said.

While card issuers might have played a big part in this crisis, I don't think they should be the only ones held responsible. Consumers like me had the option to decline any credit card offer.

Our relationship with credit card companies will soon change dramatically. The credit card law that President

Obama signed will ban many of the industry practices I just described starting in February 2010. Card issuers won't be able to raise interest rates on existing balances unless the consumer pays at least sixty days late. If the borrower is on time for the following six months, the card issuer will have to restore the original rate. No rate increases will be allowed for the first year of a credit card contract, and low introductory teaser rates will have to remain the same for six months. Banks will have to send customers their bills twenty-one days before the due date. Gone too is that confusing double-cycle billing.

The law also dictates how the companies can apply customers' payments. On cards with more than one interest rate, banks will have to apply anything above the minimum to the debt with the highest rate.

Industry officials lobbied hard against the provisions. Raising rates is how they manage risk. The changes, the card companies argued, will force them to withhold credit or raise interest rates because they won't be able to manage their risk properly. Basically what they're saying is that if they can't treat everyone differently, they'll have to treat everyone the same and go back to the early days of credit cards when each borrower got the same 18 percent interest rate.

"If the industry cannot change the pricing for people whose credit deteriorates then they have to treat most creditworthy customers the same as someone whose credit has deteriorated," said Edward L. Yingling, chief executive of the American Bankers Association. "What that means for most people is they'll pay a higher interest rate."

This debate will probably continue for years.

Hole in Your Debt

It took years of reckless, impulsive spending often brought on by stress for me to get to this point. Sometimes the stress was caused by work. More often, if was caused by heartbreak. It was a pattern I developed early in life. One afternoon, during my junior year of college, I found myself walking by a tattoo parlor. I had just broken up with a boyfriend. Without much thought, I walked in, threw down my credit card, and had the tattoo artist draw a sun on my right shoulder. During the Trejos Recovery Tour of 2007, I used my card to get a facial, manicure, pedicure, and massage at a fancy spa in Santa Monica. The task before me was daunting: How was I going to pay off that debt in a shorter amount of time than it took to build it up? And how was I going to keep myself from getting into more debt the next time I had another heartbreak, which unfortunately would probably happen given my luck with men?

Many people have gotten out—and stayed out—of debt. I needed to hear their stories.

Credit Card Success Story: Kathy M.

Kathy M. got her first credit card as a college student at Purdue University. She managed to keep her use of it under control. When she graduated she had just $500 in card debt and no student loans to pay off. She was starting her adult life on solid footing.

That didn't last long. "I went into the real world and thought certainly, I needed to live the high life. It's the typical story where I bought things and had fun and said, 'I'll pay it tomorrow.'"

By the time she was twenty-six, she had $26,000 in credit card debt and earned just $30,000 a year as a free-lance graphics and multimedia designer. What did she have to show for it? A closet full of clothing and memories of nice vacations. "In hindsight, there weren't huge line items, but I was basically funding a very upper-middle-class life-style even though I was just out of college and had no business spending that way."

It got so bad that creditors were calling her all the time. She eventually couldn't keep up with the minimum pay-ments and went into default. That's when she turned to a credit counselor. The counselor negotiated payment plans with her creditors and consolidated her debt. Each month, she sent the counseling agency about $350. For the next three years, she cut down on outings for dinner and drinks. She moved in with roommates. She reduced her shopping stints. She got a more secure job and continued to do free-lancing gigs on the side.

She did have to give up on one credit card, and the company dismissed it as a charge off. That put a blemish on her credit report for years. She managed to pay off most of her debt in the end, though.

"It was one of the most stressful times in my young life," she said.

It took a couple of years, but she eventually got a credit card again. Now thirty-four and living in Charlottesville, Virginia, the part-time writer pays off her balance right away whenever she uses her card.

"You have to get honest about your own spending and

your own responsibility in creating that situation," she said. "But also, you can't give up. It can be incredibly stressful and overwhelming, but don't give up."

Credit Card Success Story: Allison B.

Allison was raised by a single mother who didn't make that much money as a teacher but managed to make sure that her daughter had all of her financial needs met. When Allison got to the University of Michigan, she had to take care of herself. She was suddenly surrounded by students who had grown up with wealthy parents and didn't have to worry about money. She, on the other hand, was always worried about money. She was financing a good chunk of her education with loans. She decided to get a doctorate, which put her in even more debt. When she graduated, she had more than $60,000 in student loan debt. She has no regrets, though, because she is now a successful pharmacist.

What she does regret, however, is the credit card debt she accumulated as a student. Once she started making a good salary, she didn't apply it to her debt. Instead, she made a habit of going to the mall whenever she felt bored.

"I think in some ways I was making up for what I didn't have," she said. "I have friends who are facing the same kinds of things as me. I think a lot of it is, we work hard, we all have our degrees, we make good money. You see people around you who have things. You don't know what they make, but you make what you do and you must have what they have. I think it's a problem of feeling like we should have it all."

Having it all meant wearing designer clothing that didn't even fit her well. It meant buying a pair of shoes if she had a date. It meant getting expensive manicures and pedicures all the time, going out for lunch and dinner several times a week, and traveling often. In a single six-month period, she took ten trips.

"What it boiled down to was that I had no idea how I was spending my money," she said.

By the time she was twenty-eight, she decided to figure it out because she found herself owing $9,000 to three credit card issuers even though she made almost $100,000 a year and paid just $650 a month in rent. That was on top of her student loans and the $24,000 she owed for her car.

"I thought 'This is ridiculous. How am I running out of money every month?'" she said.

She cut down on the manicures and pedicures. She only shopped when she needed something. She sold her designer outfits to consignment shops. Like Kathy, she stopped eating out as often. And she got a second job teaching a university class. "It was about reprioritizing and getting passionate about something else. What I needed to be passionate about was paying down my debt."

She attacked her debt one card at a time, starting with the one with the lowest balance, which was about $700. Fortunately, that card also happened to have the highest interest rate, so she was paying off the most expensive debt first. "I started with my lowest balance just because I'm a person who is driven by seeing accomplishment," she said.

"I was able to pay off that smallest one within two months. It was such a sense of accomplishment, that instant gratification of 'Oh, I'm done.' It's almost the same feeling of instant gratification when you go shopping."

Every time she received a paycheck, she made sure she had enough for rent, utilities, and living expenses, then got online and transferred a large sum to the credit card company. Because she got paid every two weeks, that meant she was sending in two payments a month.

By mid-January 2009, she had eliminated her credit card debt and even started setting aside money in an emergency reserve fund. She stopped using her credit cards. Each time she got tempted, she reminded herself of that stress she felt when she had that debt. She also reminded herself of her long-term goals. "I want to own a house someday," the Jupiter, Florida, resident said. "I want to have enough money to have kids and not feel like I'm living paycheck to paycheck. That's my motivation, so I don't think I'm ever going to get into serious credit card debt again."

Credit Card Success Story: You

In my effort to chip away at my debt, I asked Christine for a list of her top tips. I had been meeting with her every few weeks, but she was willing to answer my questions anytime I e-mailed her. Her advice has helped me. Now I want to share some of it with you:

- Stop using credit cards to support your lifestyle. Live within your means.
- Prepare a balanced budget.

- Know what your debt is. Write down all of your credit card balances, monthly payments, and interest rates. Use the annual percentage yield (APY) to easily compare the rates to each other.
- Pay off the card with the highest interest rate first. Call your lender and ask for a lower interest rate. Make at least the minimum payment on the debt with the lower interest. Repeat that process until all the cards are paid off.
- Evaluate the advantages and disadvantages of consolidating your debt into the card with the lower interest rate.
- Establish adequate emergency savings so that you can avoid using your credit cards for unexpected expenses.
- If you are unable to manage or repay your debt, contact your lender and/or seek professional assistance. For more information, see "Fiscal Fitness: Choosing a Credit Counselor," at www.ftc.gov/bcp/edu/pubs/consumer/credit/cre26.shtm.

I also reached out to Emily Peters, who was a personal finance expert for Credit.com. She had many of the same tips, but added these:

- Put any extra money you receive, be it a bonus or a tax refund or a gift, directly toward reducing your debt.
- Look for ways to make some extra money. Have a garage sale, sell a second car, cancel your cable, etc.

- If you have good credit, try opening a new account with a good balance transfer program to reduce the interest rate on your debt.
- Evaluate your payment schedule. You can move your credit card payment dates to correspond with your paydays to make it easier to pay more.
- Use online banking programs, such as Mint.com, to easily track your progress and make payments.

Working on paying off my own credit cards was difficult enough. But there was much work to be done in other areas of my life. My credit cards, after all, were not the only reason I got into so much financial trouble. Next, I decided to explore how I had let my relationships damage my finances.

seven
love and money

Live-in Boyfriend #1 and I used to have intense discussions about any number of topics: the writings of Joseph Mitchell, the *Star Wars* trilogy, how to make the perfect flour tortilla (I certainly don't know how, but Live-in Boyfriend #1's grandmother did).

But the conversation that led to our decision to cohabitate lasted no more than a few minutes. After nearly a year of dating, he had been spending every night in my studio apartment. He had a one-bedroom not far from me but it was a messy bachelor pad. A cardboard box served as his coffee table.

One night while we were watching TV at my apartment, I said, "Why can't we live at your place? It's bigger than mine. I'm on a month-to-month lease. I can move anytime. It'll save us money."

His response: "Sure."

There was very little talk about how we were going to handle what was ultimately a financial arrangement. I didn't even know exactly what his annual salary was. All I knew was that he earned more than I did.

Money is the last thing people want to talk about when they're falling in love. But it's one of the first things they should discuss when planning their lives together. Modern relationships have become so complicated. No longer are there defined financial roles, with the husband as breadwinner and wife as homemaker. There are many more two-income households now, and you cannot automatically assume that the man is the one making the most money. There are also more financial pressures now, with so many households overloaded with debt and people losing their homes and jobs. Increasingly, people are considering a potential mate's finances before committing to a relationship. In a Money Management International survey released in February 2009, 73 percent of women chose financial security over looks when choosing a life partner, and 82 percent said financial know-how was important in a mate.

Yet so many people are dishonest to their significant others about their finances. In a Harris Interactive survey sponsored by *Redbook* magazine and Lawyers.com, 29 percent of people in a committed relationship said they have lied to their partners about their spending habits. A GfK Roper poll commissioned by the website Divorce360.com found that money is second only to verbal and physical abuse as the main reason people get divorced.

"Money is one of the top three common sources of conflict that brings couples into therapy," said Karen Osterle, a licensed psychotherapist in DC. "In fact, some people find it easier to talk about sexual matters than they do about money."

People don't always realize that when they cohabitate or marry, they are entering not only a romantic relationship but a financial partnership. There are decisions to be made. Should we have a joint bank account or keep our finances separate? Should we apply for credit cards together? How should the rent be divided? Or should we buy a house? And if we do, how should the mortgage be divided? How much should we set aside for retirement? When should we start saving for our children's educations? "The couple that plans together is much more likely to stay together," Osterle said.

In recessionary times, it is also important to come up with financial contingency plans. "What happens when someone loses his or her job? Are they prepared to do anything, take two jobs or a lesser job? Are they prepared to do what it takes to hold up their end?" said Laurie Mandel, a counselor with a private practice in Manhattan. "Don't be afraid to ask the tough questions."

As we and our mates grow old together, our finances will only get more complicated. If we don't lay the groundwork for a solid financial bond early on, we could run into trouble later. Financial differences become even more pronounced in a recession. "What comes out more strongly is that not having enough money to pay all the bills during the month is a huge source of couple distress, and for couples who are living together, it makes them less likely to get married, it makes them more likely to get divorced," said Pamela Smock, a sociology professor at the University of Michigan, who has interviewed almost 300 couples about their financial lives.

I knew my relationship with Live-in Boyfriend #1 was

in jeopardy when I opened his credit card statement one night and saw that he had taken out a cash advance. I asked him why. He said a relative needed the money. I started crying and then yelled at him. How could he do that when we had just bought a condo and needed to be more careful with money? He walked out of the condo and didn't return for hours.

My experience with Live-in Boyfriend #1 later inspired me to find a couple that was more successful at their joint financial planning than we were.

I asked Jill Foster and Sean Stickle, a DC couple in their late thirties, what the key was to their success. They said it was talking about their finances during premarital counseling a decade before.

"I said something like, 'You know what, Sean, I know it's about happiness and love, but in addition to that, we need to talk long-term about money,'" Jill said.

From then on, Jill, who is an online editor for www .womengrowbusiness.com, took charge of the finances. Sean, a computer programmer, was more than happy to relinquish that authority. "She is the financial manager of the family and to the extent that we are financially secure, it is all her doing. I contribute mostly by not screwing up," he said. Screwing up for him usually means buying too many books or forgetting to pay a bill.

The couple makes more than $100,000 a year and lives frugally in a 600-square-foot, one-bedroom rental. They have merged their bank accounts and debt. In January 2006, they had an epiphany. Despite having declared saving for retirement as their priority, they had spent $11,000 on restaurant meals the previous year.

Jill became even more of a strict financial manager. She employed Quicken to keep track of all of their expenditures. She cut their restaurant budget to $1,500 a year and enforced a rule that 12 percent of their income go into a retirement account. Her efforts did cause some tension. "I wanted to be fiscally conservative, probably to a suffocating degree, and Sean wanted to probably enjoy our money a little bit more," she said.

This is a classic case of opposites attracting, which is common when it comes to money. Many impulse buyers end up with savers. "When we partner, when we mate, we look for someone who represents the other side of the emotional coin," said Marty Tashman, a counselor in Somerset, New Jersey, who has treated many couples who feud over money.

That can wreak havoc on a relationship unless couples learn to communicate in a respectful manner. That means not shouting at your partner, as I did, when he or she makes a poor decision. There are ways to avoid conflict. Come up with a household budget together. Have a monthly money meeting and follow it up with a date so that it won't seem like a chore. But don't go overboard with the budgeting. If you have disposable income, it's okay to enjoy it as a couple every once in a while. If money becomes a source of conflict too much, counseling could help.

Unfortunately, all that I learned from talking to these counselors and advisors came too late for me and Live-in Boyfriend #1.

Home Economics

It was when we filled out a mortgage application that Live-in Boyfriend #1 and I got a clearer picture of each other's finances. It was obvious that neither one of us was as financially savvy as we should have been. That didn't stop us from buying the condo.

We made three big errors when we bought it—one we couldn't have avoided and two we could have.

The real estate market in DC had been booming for years. Properties were appreciating so quickly that people would buy condos and flip them for $50,000 profits just months later. Everyone was getting approved for mortgages and running out and buying one, two, sometimes three properties.

We would learn later that banks were artificially fueling the market by giving adjustable rate mortgages with low introductory teaser rates to people who didn't have the incomes to afford them. They were qualifying borrowers based on their ability to make the monthly payment on the teaser rate. They weren't taking into account that once the rate increased in two or three years, the borrowers would have no way of keeping up. The theory was that as long as property values went up, these people could refinance their mortgages or sell their homes at a profit.

The real estate bubble finally burst—months after we bought our condo.

Our avoidable mistake was to buy property jointly before we were married and while we were having problems. But we had been together for so long that I figured there was no way we would ever break up. When another newspaper offered him a job in another city just a few months after we bought the condo, he accepted. If we were going to get engaged, this was the time to do it. That April or May, we went to Philadelphia for a U2 concert. He asked me to marry him as Bono sang "One." I thought it an odd choice because "One" is actually not a happy love song. I think he proposed during this line: "Love is a temple, love the higher law/You ask me to enter, but then you make me crawl/And I can't be holding on to what you got, when all you got is hurt." As it turned out, it was quite apropos.

We broke up on July 4, 2005, while visiting his family. We were arguing about money and our careers. The last night I spent at his family's home, I turned to him and said, "I don't think you're ready to get married." I fell asleep angry. The next day, we drove to San Francisco where we had planned to spend a night. During the drive, he said, "You're right. I'm not ready. I'm sorry, I can't marry you."

It was the right decision, but still so painful, even more so because we had to figure out what to do with the condo. Although Live-in Boyfriend #1 had contributed nothing to the down payment, I placed his name on the mortgage. I finally got smart and insisted that we sign a contract laying out the terms of our new financial arrangement, which was to have him contribute to the mortgage until the end of 2005.

Financial advisors disagree over the wisdom of buying a home with a romantic partner you are not married to. After my own experience, I have to say I'm completely against it. I discussed this with Guy Cecala, publisher of Inside Mortgage Finance Publications. Married or not, he didn't think it made much of a difference. "Let's face it. You run the risk of getting a divorce anyway," he said.

Fair enough, but I should have had a contract drawn up *before* we bought the condo. I should have put in writing that my mother was providing the down payment as a gift, how much each of us would contribute to the monthly mortgage, and what we would do with the property in the event of a death or breakup. Not romantic, I know, but I didn't protect myself and I paid a hefty price for it.

Our final mistake was that we bought a condo we really could not afford. Between the two of us, we made about $170,000 a year, but we had other debt and we had no real savings. We should not have been allowed to buy a $375,000 condo. Our mortgage broker, however, convinced us we could afford it with an interest-only 10-year adjustable rate mortgage, which meant that none of what we paid each month would go toward the principal of the loan. I don't think she was trying to con us. She was just doing what everyone else was doing. The mortgage was completely inappropriate for us. I would learn, more than a year later while covering real estate, that such a mortgage is designed for people who expect big infusions of cash, such as bonuses at the end of the year, which they can then apply toward the principal of the loan. As journalists, we had no prospect of that. When our ten-year ARM was up, we would still owe as much as we did at the beginning of the loan. How two intelligent people allowed someone to convince them to take out such a loan, I will never figure out. But as we learned when the real estate bubble burst, many a smart person did.

Can't Buy Me Love, or Can You?

There I was, single again, after five years of what felt like a marriage. Would this be the last time my love life and financial life would intersect? Of course not.

When it comes to love, though, the money questions aren't always as heavy as whether or not to open a joint bank account or buy real estate together. Money comes into play from the very first time you go out with someone. Should the man always pay for the first date? If so, when should the woman start paying? This is particularly tricky when the economy is bad and people have less disposable income for dating.

I found myself having to learn how to date again, and I needed some advice. I asked some of my male and female friends to share their opinions.

"I'm old-fashioned, so take this with a grain of salt. The man should just about always pay, first date, second date, forever," said Jon, a graduate school student who is a year younger than I am. "The woman shouldn't pay unless and until the relationship is so normal/strong that bringing up the question seems silly. It's like the Supreme Court's pornography standard: You'll know the moment is right when you're in the moment."

Zach, a journalist who is seven years younger than I am, believes it depends largely on who does the inviting. "If the man asks, he should pay. If the woman asks, she should. In either case, the 'guest' should offer to split, but this offer should be rejected. So if Man asks Woman out, then Woman should offer to split, but Man should say 'don't be silly' and pay for all."

In Zach's opinion, if the man constantly does the inviting and paying, the woman should "offer something else gently—movie tickets, the dessert, etc." If the man and woman start dating regularly, they should rotate the paying of dates, unless there's a serious economic disparity between the two. The dates should also vary in terms of expense. There should be a mix of picnics, expensive dinners, activity dates, cook-at-home dinners, etc.

Mitch, a journalist a year older than I am who lives with his fiancée, said that during his single days, he would always pick up the check on the first date. "If a girl offered to split the first date cost and seemed like she would be offended if you didn't let her split it, then I might split it," he said. "That never happened, but if it did I would have thought about it."

What happens after that is up to the couple, he said. He paid the first few times he went out with his fiancée. She offered to pay or split the bill, but he turned her down because he wanted to impress her. Now that they're living together and have pretty much all of their meals together, they split a lot of the costs, unless he's organizing a special date night, in which case, he picks up the tab. His fiancée also occasionally treats him to special meals.

Now let's see what the ladies had to say.

"Money and dating is an awkward topic, but generally I think the guy should pay for the first few dates," Erica, three years younger than I am, said. "It depends, though. If you're both in school or if one person makes a lot more money than the other, then obviously sometimes that doesn't work out. But yes, in general, I think the guy should pay for the first few dates."

Once past the introductory dates, Erica argues that the woman should start covering some expenses, but that the man should always pay just a little bit more often. "So the guy pays 70 percent of the time and the woman pays 30 percent," she said.

Victoria, who is my age, has a more irreverent take on this. I asked her this question the day after she watched a Chris Rock standup routine on cable. "He says, 'If you want to dry up her [insert vulgar word for female reproductive organ here], then you let her pay,'" she e-mailed to me.

All kidding aside, she had this to say: "We are independent and self-sufficient women, but a date is traditional and I think at least in the beginning he should try. Doesn't mean high-end restaurants all the time. Every situation is different."

But if he makes substantially more than the woman, "he better pay or he is out. If he is a student, you might not expect it because you know he is broke, and this is understood. But I would be leery of a man who wants to go Dutch on the first date."

I thought back to the first man I was with after Live-in Boyfriend #2. Eager to wipe out the memory of Live-in Boyfriend #2, I went out with this man just a week after the breakup. Let's call him Rebound Guy. The morning after he spent a night at my place, Rebound Guy and I walked from my apartment to my favorite coffeehouse. We walked up to the counter and each ordered a skim chai. He asked the cashier for a scone. The cashier rang it up and told us the total. I turned to Rebound Guy, expecting him to treat me to a chai. He did not reach for his wallet. I then pulled out mine and handed money to the cashier. "Thank you," Rebound Guy said.

I almost wrote him off, but he insisted on coming over to my apartment and making me dinner the following weekend. I decided to give him a chance. He showed up with a bag of groceries then whipped up a salad, fish, and some sort of side dish. For dessert, he presented me with berries and two types of sorbet. We had a fun evening. I once again let him spend the night. The next morning, after we said our good-byes, he walked into my kitchen and packed up the leftover sorbet. That was it for me. Not only had he not bought me breakfast after I let him spend a night at my place, but he couldn't even leave me with a pint of sorbet.

Perhaps I was being too picky. Why did I feel entitled to free meals from a man just because he's a man? Or perhaps I just didn't want to give him a chance because I was clearly not over my breakup. Either way, he was not the right guy for me. One of my friends dubbed him Big Spender. I started ignoring Big Spender's calls and text messages soon after the dinner.

Dana, a journalist my age, had a more equitable approach to dating. "My philosophy is, first date, I want to be treated, but I will pay for the drinks afterwards," she said. She has one exception, however: "If I insist on sharing the dinner bill, the message is: You won't see me again my dear, so at least I will have the decency to pay for my food."

Incidentally, Dana's pay-if-you-want-to-go-home-early tactic is pretty common. How the bill is handled the first time says a lot about whether or not there will be a second time.

"When the man doesn't offer to pay for the whole thing, the woman tends not to like him as much. If the woman doesn't offer to pay her half, the man tends to not like her as much," said Mary Gresham, an Atlanta psychologist who specializes in money management. "If the man likes her and she likes him, she usually lets him pick up the whole thing. If she doesn't like him, she usually pays her half because she doesn't want to have an obligation to him. None of the messages are very clear and none of them are very straight. There's a lot of mix-up."

TRUE.com, an online relationship service, addressed this topic in its survey of 2,286 men and women. Less than 1 percent of women felt they should pick up the tab for the first date, while 78 percent of men considered it their duty to pay. That said, a quarter of the women said they would be willing to split the bill with the man, and 22 percent said that whoever did the asking out should cover the check.

I agree with most of what my friends had to say. In recent decades, women have enjoyed a rising level of independence and parity in the workplace and in their love lives. That doesn't mean they want chivalry to die. Generally, women want to be wooed. Treating a woman to a nice meal is one way of wooing. If I know the man I am dating makes a lot more money than I do, I have no problem letting him pay the majority of the time. I will always show my gratitude, and I will try to reciprocate in other ways, either by buying him a drink or an occasional gift or cooking for him. (One of my ex-flings, a journalist and now a buddy, pointed out that men can do this too. While he was an unemployed graduate school student, he dated a woman who had a high-paying job. She paid for most meals and drinks. But, he said, she received "ample compensation." I didn't ask him what form that came in.)

Some of these issues come up with gay dating too. There, I think, it's not a question about gender (obviously) and more a question of age and income.

I do realize, with either gay or straight dating, that at some point if you never pay for a single meal, you might run the risk of becoming a sugar baby.

Live-in Boyfriend #1 was all about the chivalry. He always opened doors for me, and he never let me pay for any of our restaurant meals. For every birthday, Christmas, and Valentine's Day, he got me the same thing: A gift card to a clothing store because he knew how much I loved to shop. It got so ridiculous that one night, as I was walking home from a party with Emily and our friend Justin Blum, they began to tease me. They changed the lyrics of the Destiny's Child song "Independent Woman" from "The shoes on my feet/I've bought it/The clothes I'm wearin'/I've bought it" and serenaded me with "The shoes on your feet/[Live-in Boyfriend #1] bought it. The clothes you're wearin'/[Live-in Boyfriend #1] bought it."

After I broke up with Live-In Boyfriend #2, I had a regular but not very serious involvement with another writer.

He was younger but made more money than I did, so he often paid for our outings. One morning, as I was leaving his apartment, I realized I did not have enough cash for a cab and asked him for some, even though I could have easily walked a few blocks to an ATM. He handed me a $10 bill. It was understood that I would not have to pay him back, and I didn't. But taking cash from a man felt a lot different than letting him buy me dinner. An image of Ricky Ricardo giving Lucy a wad of money to buy a dress popped into my head.

As it turns out, hard economic times are prompting many women to turn to men to help them with their finances, as evidenced by the growing popularity of websites such as SeekingArrangement.com and SugarDaddie .com, which match sugar daddies with their sugar babies. I would never go that far. But had I gone far enough to qualify as an embarrassment to the women's liberation movement? Had I developed a pattern of letting men take care of me financially?

I consulted with Kathleen Burns Kingsbury, a licensed mental health counselor. She said there's no right way to handle the payment of dates, but that you have to do "what you're comfortable with."

But you also have to be comfortable with your ability to pay your own way. "I feel very strongly that for women, especially in their 20s and 30s, they need to know their value and worth and they need to be able to care for themselves," Kingsbury said. "We will have to manage our finances and we will be alone in doing it. We live longer."

My mother has succeeded at this, but she admits that

it took her a long time. When she and my dad first got together, she let him assume the dominant financial role, partly because he made more money and partly because her own father was so clearly the head of their household when she was growing up. As she grew older, and more comfortable standing up to my father, she realized that she was just as good or even better than he was at managing money. She got her own bank account and started tucking away her own money, and declared that she did not need any of his. It was quite an extraordinary shift given that she was raised to believe that women need men and their money.

My planner had made me jot down my short-term and long-term financial goals. As I looked back at all my relationships with men, I added one more to the list: No more accepting cash from men.

eight
to have or have not

One of my most embarrassing moments as a personal finance writer was at Georgetown Park, a popular mall in DC, where I went to search for people to interview for a story about compulsive shopping. It was sometime in June 2008, around the time I had to ask my parents for a loan. I had been avoiding malls because I did not want to spend any more money on dresses and shoes and handbags. For several weeks, I had been quite successful. But here I was, forced back to the mall. This assignment was bringing me face-to-face with my own shopping demons.

In an effort to stay out of the actual shops, I kept to the open areas and food court, approaching anyone with lots of shopping bags. But when I saw the cute sundresses on display at J.Crew, I caved. Their tank dresses and halter tops are always so tasteful and flattering. Then I veered toward Anthropologie. The candles looked and smelled great. The lamps were adorable and the rugs funky. The dresses were creative and looked like they would be perfect for a short girl like me. Unfortunately, I didn't find any dress I liked for less than $148. I left and hit H&M, which I reasoned was safer because of their affordable prices. They had cute empire waist tops for less than $20. Still, I was not going to buy anything, I repeated in my head. Thankfully, I didn't find anything that I thought was worth the guilt I knew would follow any purchase. I did, however, find a couple of people to interview. As I walked out, I passed by the White House/Black Market. That's when the trouble began. I don't normally like strapless dresses, but the ones on display had such pretty floral patterns that even they called out to me. The halter tops, drape-necks, and scoop-necks were just as appealing.

I have two shopping fetishes. One is coats. I probably have a dozen of them. My coworker and friend Annie once proclaimed: "You have more coats than God. But I guess God doesn't really need any coats." I apparently do. The other is black dresses. Some people might call that boring, but I stand by my theory: Pair a cute little black dress with interesting shoes and an exotic scarf or necklace, and you've got yourself a simple, elegant, always flattering outfit. This was not the season for coat shopping. Cute black dresses, however, are as easy to find as a quart of milk. And I found a fantastic one, in the window of White House/Black Market. It was short enough to show off my legs, which were looking good at that point after many months of spinning class three or four times a week. Because I had shopped there before and let the store send me a catalog each month, I got a 10 percent discount.

When I walked back into the office, my editor asked if I had scored any good interviews. "Yes," I replied.

He knew how much I liked to shop and how much I was trying to abstain.

"You didn't buy anything, did you?"

I blushed and made a quick exit.

My editor and friends laughed about it, but I soon realized how extreme shopping is not the least bit funny.

That realization came when I got on the phone with Sharon, who at the time was thirty-six. Her shopping habit had left her with $35,000 in credit card debt and a counseling appointment.

"When I'm unhappy, I want to shop to make myself happy," she said. "I'm happy for a brief moment and then angry with myself because I've spent money."

I heard a bit of myself in Sharon, and I'm clearly not alone. According to a study in the *American Journal of Psychiatry*, 5.8 percent of Americans are compulsive buyers, grabbing things they don't need or can't afford to the point that it affects their relationships, their finances, and their health. Even mounting bills aren't enough to keep some hard-core shopaholics from spending money on clothing, vacations, or meals at fine restaurants. You would think that an economic downturn and unstable job market would have more of an impact. But it can actually encourage such behavior, triggering a self-perpetuating cycle: The more stressed out shopaholics get about money, the greater the urge to shop as a way of decompressing.

"For people already in the throes of addiction, the economy tanking is just another stressor," said Terry Shulman, a Detroit therapist who runs the Shulman Center for Compulsive Theft and Spending. "It's no different than the alcoholic afraid of losing a job or money, but they're still drinking. I think particularly if people feel, 'I'm not going to have a retirement fund, I'm not going to be able to afford the house of my dreams, then I'm going to get nice things, clothing, electronics.'"

For a time, easy credit, aggressive advertising by retailers, and the availability of goods on the Internet made compulsive buying much easier. It cuts across gender lines and is more common among those making less than $50,000 a year, according to the study in the *American Journal of Psychiatry*. It is so widespread that the American Psychiatric Association has for years been discussing including compulsive buying in its manual of mental disorders, which it plans to finish updating by 2012.

While there is no data showing whether compulsive shopping has increased, psychiatrists said they are treating more people who are struggling with it.

"In the past, patients with compulsive shopping problems may have had shame and humiliation and certainly would not tell their spouses or psychologists," said Eric Hollander, chairman of psychiatry at the Mount Sinai School of Medicine, who has written about the topic. "Now, there is an increased focus on compulsive shopping."

It is not an easy problem to solve because shopping is so ingrained in the American psyche. It is an American pastime. Want proof of this national obsession with material goods? Just flip through *Us Weekly* or watch the *Sex and the City* movie. The cultural messages and instructions we get from *Sex and the City* and the like is that our self-worth is linked to what we buy. This goes back a long way in social history. Ours is a capitalist society driven by a consumer culture. From early times, people bartered goods in markets. Then shops became fixtures of communities. Then came the supermarket in 1930, and later, in the 1950s, the shopping mall. Now, there are many ways to shop that don't even require you to leave your home. You can order merchandise from catalogs, from the Home Shopping Network, and now, pretty much anywhere, online. There is demand for these services. We want what we see on TV. We want what our classmates are wearing. We want what our neighbors have. That has been slowly changing in the last year because the recession has made frugality chic. But once the economy improves we will likely go back to trying to keep up with the Joneses.

"It's the ideology of America that you are what you own," said Lorrin Koran, a professor of psychiatry at Stanford University's medical school, who coauthored the 2006 *American Journal of Psychiatry* study. "You're encouraged to identify yourself and value yourself based on what you own or buy or display."

That's why Steven, a student at the University of the District of Columbia, is on the hunt for Black Label hats, Nike sneakers, and LRG T-shirts pretty much every weekend. When I found him before the economy got really bad, he was scouring the racks of Filene's Basement for brand names. "You have to look a certain way," he said. "I'm a big fashion fanatic. I have, like, 200 pairs of shoes."

He does not consider himself a compulsive shopper, but in his quest for the right look, he admits to at least being an impulsive shopper. Twice, he was late paying his cell phone bill because he miscalculated and shopped a bit too much. "If I see something I like and no one else is wearing it, I'm going to get it," he said.

Sharon too would get a high every time she found something that no one else had. She dressed so well that her coworkers nicknamed her the "princess." She loved being the fashionista at work because, she readily admitted, it was a boost to her low self-esteem.

Her shopping addiction started in college with her first credit card. She was tired of owning just one pair of tennis shoes, so she quickly filled her closet with Gucci, Coach, and Louis Vuitton items.

"I wanted to fit in," she said. "I was tired of looking like a boy."

Over the years, shopping became a daily habit. When she had two children, she turned her attention to their wardrobe. She bought them expensive clothing because she didn't want their classmates to make fun of them. By age five, her daughter was wearing $80 Lelli Kelly shoes.

"It doesn't stop there," she said. "Every holiday, I want her to have a beautiful dress. For Easter, her birthday, Thanksgiving, or Christmas, I want her to have something that is unusual."

Sharon realized she needed help when her daughter complained of not having enough clothing. Her part-time job at a health insurance company was not sustaining her habit. So she canceled her credit cards, found a debt consultant, and called Shulman, the Detroit therapist.

I can see how Sharon got herself into this mess. My parents always made sure my siblings and I had plenty of food, a good education, and enough clothing. But their idea of enough was not mine. As a teenager, I would watch TV shows such as *Beverly Hills 90210* and envy Jennie

Garth and Shannen Doherty for their looks and wardrobe. But my parents couldn't afford to satiate my shopping appetite. When I went to the mall, my mom would usually hand me $20, sometimes $40 if she had it to spare. It was never enough for what I wanted to buy.

When I got a credit card, I was able to dress better. Not many people dress up in newsrooms, so when I wore a flattering dress or a skirt with an unusual pattern and knee-high boots, I'd get compliments. It was, as Sharon said, a boost to my self-esteem. Was I too a shopaholic? How healthy was it that getting noticed for my skirts made me feel good about myself? Was I really a personal finance writer with a shopping problem?

Donald Black, a professor of psychiatry at the University of Iowa and an expert on compulsive shopping, says the first step to dealing with unhealthy shopping habits is to admit to the problem. Next, he encourages people who binge-buy to get rid of their credit cards and checkbooks. Then he urges them to find other hobbies to replace shopping and produce a different kind of high, such as that from running. If they've gotten into serious debt, they should seek counseling from a financial institution, planner, or credit-counseling agency. Joining a support group such as Debtors' Anonymous might also help. Sometimes compulsive shopping is coupled with a disorder such as obsessive-compulsive disorder. In those cases, medication could be warranted.

I was happy to hear this news: Compulsive shoppers don't have to stop shopping for good. But when they do shop, they shouldn't do it alone, and they shouldn't do it with other shopaholics. "The idea is they're much less likely to shop impulsively with friends or spouses," Black said.

After talking to all these mental health experts, I concluded that I had to deal with my own shopping problem. It had not gotten so out of hand that I couldn't go weeks without shopping. When I didn't have the money, I would more often than not refrain from buying something. Shopping has not affected my ability to work. It has not ruined my relationships. But it has certainly left me with a smaller bank account. I need to exert more self-control, which is something Christine, my planner, has helped me do. She has taught me how to prioritize my needs. If I buy another dress it would take away from money I could spend on traveling, and I would much rather take a trip than add to my black dress collection. I get e-mails every day from Neiman Marcus, Ann Taylor, Apple—every store I've ever walked into, it seems—notifying me of a sale or offering a coupon. Since I've started budgeting, I've immediately deleted them so I don't feel the urge to buy something just because it's on sale. "Good for you," Christine said when I told her this.

Now, when I am tempted to buy something, I ask myself, "Do I really need this?" Usually, the answer is no. I can't say I've been successful every time, but I've gotten much better.

Oddly enough, I found another person whose career you would think would keep her from developing an addiction. When I talked to her in the beginning of 2009, Talia Witowski was a twenty-nine-year-old Los Angeles psychotherapist who spent years counseling people with eating disorders and other addictions. At the same time, she was battling her own compulsion to shop. "I was leading a severely double life," she said. "I spent five years working with addicts. I could see it in them but I couldn't see it in me."

It began, as these things do, when she was a teenager. Her grandmother gave her cash gifts, which she spent right away on things she can't even recall now. The older she got, the more money went for clothing, shoes, and works of art. When she ran out of cash, she ran up credit card debt. "I couldn't hold on to money," she said. "I liked things, I liked being able to get things. It's like a hit, using a drug or having a drink or smoking a cigarette."

By 2007, she was also drinking alcohol to feel better. She didn't realize she had a problem until she escorted one of her patients, a girl with bulimia, to the hospital. That's where she met a counselor who would later become her spiritual mentor, helping her realize how unhappy she was and how worthless she felt. Through counseling, writing, meditating, and praying, she has been able to stop drinking and change her shopping behavior. She now has a budget and buys only what she needs—and at less expensive stores.

There is no way to cure people of an addiction to shopping, but the psychiatrists I talked to assured me that shopaholics could certainly learn to manage it.

This was good to hear. At some point in the remaining fifty or so years of my life, I will once again need a new dress or pair of shoes. What I need to do, what we all need to do, is to become intelligent shoppers. There are people out there—not necessarily wealthier people—who have figured out how to own pretty things without getting into debt. I reached out to some, many of them my friends, for advice.

Diversify. And I'm Not Talking About Stocks.

Christina is a thirtysomething federal employee who always stands out at parties because she has a unique sense of style. Her dresses are always colorful, her jewelry exotic, her handbags original. When I took her out for drinks to learn her shopping secrets, she showed up in a $30 aqua green vintage dress, a Gucci bag she bought at a discount online, an African necklace from a flea market, and black suede boots from Aerosole, known for high quality at affordable prices.

"You can get fabulous things, eclectic things, collector's items, and it doesn't have to cost a ton," she said as we sipped our white wine.

She has a friend who spent $900 on a Dolce & Gabbana tank top. "I can probably have ten or fifteen vintage dresses with that amount of money," she said.

Christina never buys anything with money she doesn't have. When she got out of graduate school, she decided she was going to look good on a pay-as-you-go system. "It's a lifestyle choice," she said.

She and her husband splurge on two big trips a year, but to do so they sacrifice things like a big flat-screen TV. Christina then uses their trips as shopping expeditions. Jewelry is often a lot cheaper overseas. She also has picked up inexpensive dresses in places like Bali.

Back home, she prefers vintage clothing stores and consignment shops. You can find high-end items there for a fraction of their original cost, and often, they are barely used. Once you've scouted out some great shops in your area, get to know the owners and employees, Christina advised. If you have a particular item in mind, ask them to be on the lookout for it and follow up regularly.

Also, seek creative places to shop. In graduate school, Christina found unusual pieces of jewelry on the Home Shopping Network and through infomercials on late-night TV. "Are you kidding?" I asked her. Almost everything I've seen advertised on TV has been tacky. Have you ever seen the infomercial for the Snuggie, a blanket with sleeves that keeps you warm while you reach for the remote control? Christina insisted you could find some quality merchandise on TV. "They buy in bulk so it's cheap," she said. "It's you and the old grandmas in Sarasota watching. But it doesn't matter."

Don't snub stores that have a reputation for inexpensive merchandise either. Check out Forever 21 and H&M. The items might not last years but they are trendy, so you don't need them to last a long time. Don't, however, wear Forever 21 alone.

"Diversify," Christina said. I laughed. As a personal finance writer, I only used that word when writing about stocks.

"If you have a good sense of style, it doesn't have to be expensive. You mix things," she said. "If you have an H&M dress with lots of color, pair it with expensive jewelry or a handbag."

Recessionize

Next, I reached out to Annie, who owns seven cashmere sweaters, none of which she bought for more than $50. She is a big proponent of thrift stores, which many people shy away from because it takes a lot of digging to find anything good. But in recent years, Annie has concluded that the products have improved. It was at a thrift store that she found a purple cashmere sweater with three-quarter-length sleeves, originally from Macy's, for just $3.49. Her biggest coup was a $1,300 Alexander McQueen blazer that cost her $39. She also patronizes consignment stores, which she admits tend to have higher quality items than the thrifts.

Recessionizing your wardrobe has apparently become the in thing to do. When the National Association of Resale & Thrift Shops surveyed shopkeepers in mid-2009, it found that sales were up from the previous year at 64 percent of their stores. Annie was ahead of this trend and has a much healthier bank account because of it.

Another one of Annie's tricks: Buy winter clothes in the summer and summer clothes in the winter, and never, ever buy anything around Christmastime. She once scored a cashmere pashmina for $75, half the price, because she bought it in July. "Who's going to buy a cashmere wrap in July?" she asked.

Annie is also a big fan of eBay, with one caveat: Don't turn to it for designer items unless you really know the brand because you could end up with knockoffs. Better to try Bluefly.com or Yoox.com. Other friends suggested Bagborroworsteal.com, which lets you rent designer handbags. Or try Google's Froogle shopping search engine.

Type in the product you are looking for and Google will find where it is being sold and sort it by price.

If you want to stick with conventional stores such as Banana Republic, J.Crew or Ann Taylor, Raquel Vincent, a twentysomething New Yorker who blogs about fashion and beauty, advises against buying anything at full price. "It will always go on sale," she said. That's especially true now that there's a recession and consumer spending has nosedived. Stores are desperate to get rid of merchandise that has been lingering for too long. Most offer special deals, such as coupons or free shipping, if you shop online.

Laura Yoder, the thirtysomething owner and creator of 24-7 Style, loves shopping but cannot afford big-name brands. "You have to decide between being a label-lover or a smart shopper," she said. "Given my current financial status, it's not really a good idea for me to buy a pair of Louboutins, although someday I have no doubt I'll have a pair or two."

Last winter, she bought an ombré-striped turtleneck from Kmart for $6.49. Each time she wore it, she received compliments. "People are so concerned with labels and brands, that they aren't realizing great items can be found for less at the 'Marts,' as I call them—Kmart and Wal-Mart. These stores are really working on bringing consumers affordable fashion."

You can also find classy pieces at places like Target, Marshall's, and Filene's Basement.

Many of these tips apply to men as well (okay, not the ones about handbags, but you can find clothing at most of the places I just mentioned.) At the risk of sounding stereotypical, however, I will offer some advice on buying electronics. This applies to the ladies as well; iPods, after all, are gender-neutral.

First of all, consider shopping online. In *Consumer Reports'* 2008 reader survey, the highest-rated electronics retailers were Amazon.com and Crutchfield.com. Many are reluctant to go this route because they don't want to pay for shipping or worry that the items are too delicate to travel. But *Consumer Reports* found that most retailers are willing to throw in free shipping, and there were very few reports of damage. Just be sure to avoid expensive accessories or extended warranties.

Many websites such as Crutchfield.com, WarehouseDeals .com, and Amazon.com offer refurbished or open box items that have been returned by the customer and restored by the manufacturer. *Consumer Reports* said these are worth it if you can save at least 30 percent and if you can trust the manufacturer or retailer.

Finally, never be afraid to negotiate, when you first buy the item and even after you've taken it home. I have friends who bought items at a store only to find it on sale just weeks later. They returned to the retailer and asked for that discount. The retailer was willing to do it as long as they had the receipt. Remember: Always know your store's return policy, and keep your receipts for at least thirty days.

It's Not Just About the Buying

When we think about clothing, bags, shoes, or electronics, we always think about spending. But you can actually make money off what you have in your closet or home.

Every summer and winter, my friend Elham goes through her closet and pulls out items she no longer wants or wears. She puts them in two piles: For charity and for resale. She takes the tax deduction for the clothing she donates. High-end items she tries to sell on eBay. Lower-end items she takes to a consignment store. She once bought a Diane von Furstenberg dress on sale at Neiman Marcus for $110. Original price: $350. She sold it on eBay for $200.

Annie used to make hundreds of extra dollars a month selling her great finds from thrift and consignment stores. She once bought an Yves Saint Laurent Rive Gauche dress for $120 and sold it on eBay for $130. That's not much of a profit but think about it: She made $10 for wearing the dress.

Getting paid to wear a dress is the kind of addiction you can really get into.

nine
you're so vain

I blame my obsession with Bulgari on the Wanderer.

Somehow, I went from being perfectly happy using Head & Shoulders as a teenager in Queens to ordering Lush shampoo online after discovering it in a London store a few years ago. I admit it. I became vain. I like getting manicures, pedicures, and facials. Having glowing skin and soft hair just makes me feel good.

But the Wanderer unintentionally took my love of fine cosmetics to a new level. I can't tell you who the Wanderer is because I promised him I would not. I can tell you that I met him at a dinner party overseas. I was immediately attracted to him. But I had a boyfriend so I never pursued anything.

When the boyfriend and I broke up, I shamelessly e-mailed the Wanderer, even though I had not spoken to him in months. I told him about the breakup. We e-mailed back and forth a little but nothing much came of it.

A few months later, in summer 2007, the Wanderer showed up in DC. He ran into a friend of mine and somehow my name came up. The Wanderer told my friend to tell me to e-mail him. It was up to me to make the first move. I contemplated this. Did I really want to get involved with someone who doesn't even live in the same country? Was I developing a pattern of getting involved with unavailable men? Okay, I already had a pattern, and in I plunged. (We actually started spending time together quite regularly afterward, but given that he wanders the world and is in no rush to settle down, I have kept him in the unavailable category.)

After our dinner date, we left the restaurant, walking arm in arm, in search of a quiet place to have a nightcap. I don't remember who suggested it, but we decided to have the nightcap at his hotel—the Ritz Carlton. We went straight to his room, ordered a bottle of wine, and stayed up for hours, wrapped in oversized bathrobes, talking, drinking, and, well, getting to know each other. It was decadent.

The most decadent part, however, came the next morning when I got into the shower and reached for the shampoo. It was Bulgari. I had never smelled anything like it. I found this description of it online: "a delicate bouquet of ambrette, white pepper, musk, woody amber and white tea." I didn't even know what all of that meant, but it sounded like a magical potion. I was hooked.

Unfortunately, Bulgari shampoo is not cheap, as I learned later when the sample bottle was empty and I went to Bloomingdale's with my girlfriends to buy some of my own. A 6.7 ounce bottle cost nearly $50 with tax. I opened it to let my companions get a whiff of that delightful scent. My French friend Daphne, who knows much more about fragrances than I do, also walked away with a bottle. Since then, it has become a running joke among my friends. Daphne got me a bottle for my thirty-second birthday. Friends have stayed at the Ritz and returned with Ziploc bags filled with Bulgari sample products for me.

Okay, I know my obsession with Bulgari is over the top. But if you're reading this, you probably have your own beauty product addictions. I'm not just talking to the women out there. Many men spend just as much time as we do grooming. (By the way, Bulgari makes a shampoo and shower gel especially for men.) The pressure to look good is so much greater for us than it was for our parents' generation. You turn on the TV or go to the movies and all the actors have great skin and hair, unless they are playing characters with bad skin and hair, in which case they go on to win Emmys or Oscars.

The cosmetics industry has fed off—and fed—this obsession with beauty. More than 11 billion personal care products are sold each year, according to the Personal Care Products Council, which represents the cosmetics, toiletries, and fragrance industry. We live in a society where La Mer can charge $2,100 for 1.5 ounces of skin cream. "The American culture is about excess. Everyone has an excessive amount of clothes, shoes, purses, and their makeup bags reflect this as well," said Lyndsey M. Yeager, a professional makeup artist and owner of Glossa studio in suburban Cincinnati.

It is so easy to get carried away. My worst transgression was in July 2008, when I went to Chicago for a journalism convention. After three nights of little sleep and lots of eating and drinking, my skin was dehydrated and my eyes were surrounded by dark circles. One afternoon, my friend Terry and I took a stroll down Michigan Avenue. I foolishly let this tall, handsome, well-groomed PR guy lead me into Neiman Marcus. I told myself I wouldn't spend any money. I had only just started to recover from the disastrous month in which I had to borrow money from my parents. But as I walked by the cosmetics counter, a salesperson offered me a sample of eye cream. There was a party to attend that night, and I wanted to look good. I sat in the makeup chair as she rubbed Orlane cream around my eyes.

"Do you use any antiaging cream?" she asked me.

"No," I replied. "I'm only thirty-one."

"It's never too early to start using antiaging cream," she said, her hands on her hips.

"She's right," Terry, my enabler, said.

"Do you use this stuff?" I asked him.

"Of course," he said. "My wife and I both do." I have to admit that they both look good.

Before I knew it, I had applied for a Neiman Marcus card and charged $445 worth of cleanser, toner, and eye contour cream. I even got bronzer because I liked the way it looked on my shoulders. I walked out feeling guilty but looking good. Terry tried to justify my impulse buy. "You have to invest in your skin," he said.

Is this really an investment worth making?

It turns out that often when we buy those expensive creams, lotions, and toners, we are paying a lot for packaging, marketing, and celebrity endorsements. The cosmetics companies charge a lot because they can. People add their names to waiting lists to buy the latest creations by La Mer,

La Prairie, and Orlane. They are wowed by the sounds of the ingredients. Indeed, cosmetics companies have gotten more creative with their concoctions, using ingredients such as sea kelp, fish roe extracts, and gold particles. In 2008, the *International Cosmetic Ingredient Dictionary*, published by the Personal Care Products Council, had more than 15,000 ingredients in it. In 1994, it had just 6,000.

The companies say they have special patent formulas and tout their own research, which is hardly ever published in any peer review journal. Cosmetics are not as tightly regulated as prescription drugs. The Food and Drug Administration prohibits the companies from claiming to cure a disease or to change the function of the body in any way, and there are several laws governing product safety. But it seems to me that the agency only really intervenes if there is a widespread problem with the product once it hits the shelves.

So when you put on your moisturizing lotion, you can trust that it probably won't harm your body. But you can't be sure it will produce the effects you want it to. "You can get the smelly good stuff. You can go out and get all the fancy [products] and the lip balm and lip enhancers, but there's no study showing they are better," said Dr. Craig A. Vander Kolk, professor of plastic surgery at Johns Hopkins University School of Medicine.

In 2007, *Consumer Reports* tested antiwrinkle cream and moisturizers on 200 women between the ages of thirty and seventy. For twelve weeks, researchers monitored their wrinkle depth and skin roughness and asked them their personal opinions. The researchers found that the high-priced products weren't necessarily better than their cheaper counterparts. In fact, the top performer was Procter & Gamble's Olay three-piece Regenerist collection, which comes with Enhancing Lotion, Perfecting Cream, and Regenerating Serum, and cost about $60. It was rated higher than a similar La Prairie Cellular line, which had a $335 price tag. But the study found that even the top-performing creams reduced wrinkles by less than 10 percent.

So are we better off just drinking lots of water and using sunscreen every day?

This is a matter of huge debate among my girlfriends, as I learned during brunch one Sunday at Elham's house.

"You don't go cheap. It's your skin," Daphne, who is my age, declared very emphatically.

She then went on to tell us that one Saturday night she got home from a party and turned on her TV. A commercial for a line of Cindy Crawford beauty products was on. She doesn't know if it was the wine or the commercial that convinced her to pick up the phone and order $140 worth of cleansers and creams.

"Buying something from Cindy Crawford is quite cheesy," she opined. Drinking and dialing is also not advisable, I pointed out. But to her surprise, the products seemed to work. The creams were light and refreshing, and she quickly noticed an improvement in her skin.

Elham, a twentysomething who manages to look and dress great on a strict budget, vehemently argued against expensive products.

"Just do Oil of Olay—$25 at CVS," she said. "There's no sense in spending $180 for a small bottle."

This is a woman who buys shampoo in bulk at Costco. She gets deals on beauty products on Drugstore.com. She shampoos her hair with an egg yolk every once in a while to add protein and body. (If you do that, please rinse with cold, not warm, water. Otherwise you'll end up with scrambled eggs in your hair.) Lip scrubs? Nonsense, she said. They cost $15 at a spa when all you have to do is mix sugar and Vaseline. The sugar exfoliates while the Vaseline moisturizes. "Learn how to do things yourself," she said.

Both Daphne and Elham have beautiful skin and hair. Who was I to disbelieve?

I thought back to my beloved Bulgari shampoo. It certainly makes my hair smell good. But had it done anything to the quality of my hair that Herbal Essences had not? I can't say it had.

"It all depends on the person and how they feel using that product. Skin care and makeup are personal and it is the feeling that you get from using those products that makes all of the difference in the world," said Jennifer Walsh, a beauty industry insider and chief executive of Behind The Brand Media.

In other words, you don't HAVE to spend a lot of money to look good. If you have a lot of disposable income and you want that $300 cream because it makes your skin glow, by all means, go for it. But for those of you on a tight budget, I asked some beauty experts and people my age to reveal their secrets.

Staying Stunning on the Cheap

The first thing to do is assess your needs. I have at least a dozen bottles of body lotion of various sizes in my bathroom. I have at least three bottles of hand lotion and two of foot lotion. Yet every time I walk into a cosmetics store, I want to buy more. I'll see a strawberry pomegranate body cream and think, I don't have anything with a strawberry scent, and pomegranates have antioxidant powers. Since I started budgeting, I've learned to tell myself to use what I have and only buy what I need. It's a major act of willpower but you can do it. Once you do that, you can then shop intelligently for what you can't go without.

- *Do your research.* Learn about ingredients. It could keep you from buying products with ingredients that won't do you any good. For instance, said Yeager, if you've got extremely dry hair, look for a product with Royal Jelly or Vitamin E, both known for moisturizing.
- *Find dual uses for items.* Take cleanser. You can find some that also serve as makeup removers and toners. Neutrogena One Step Gentle Cleanser, for instance, will run you only $6.20 for a 5.2 ounce bottle.
- *Don't be afraid to ask for freebies.* Go to any makeup counter and ask for samples of cosmetics, skin-care products, and fragrances. Many websites such as Sephora.com and Beauty.com offer samples with purchases. Call the consumer hotlines of a number of larger cosmetic companies and request any samples they have available. Emphasize that you are likely

to purchase the item if you like it, and chances are many of the companies will send it to you.

- *Try baby skin care lines.* They are usually cheaper and just as good as the adult lines. Check out Johnson & Johnson, Mustela, and Aveeno products.
- *Shop online.* Sometimes you can find high-end cosmetics on eBay or Amazon. Many people will sell unopened beauty products or a collection of samples. Also check out Drugstore.com.
- *No need to give it up, but do scale back.* I won't give up my manicures and pedicures. But for a while, I was going once a week. There's no need for that. For one thing, pedicures can last a long time. I only get one a month now. In the winter, I wait longer to get a pedicure. How many people are going to see your bare feet? Also, you don't have to have a full-on manicure each time you go. Opt for a cheaper polish change. Or go natural. There's nothing wrong with that as long as you moisturize your fingers and refrain from biting your nails.
- *Befriend the people behind the counter.* If you have a favorite makeup store, keep going back to the same salesperson. She might be willing to do a free makeover. At the very least, she'll give you some good tips if you ask.
- *Don't go for trendy colors.* Cosmetics are just as faddish as clothing. Remember the MAC Hello Kitty collection? Probably not. You should really think about what colors will suit your lifestyle, skin tone, and career.

No More Bad Hair Days

Hair is so important. It's one of the first things people notice about you. There is so much that can go wrong with your hair, from a bad cut to frizz. If you want to avoid having to wear a cap or pulling your hair up into a ponytail every day, try this:

- *Mix up your shampoo.* If you really need to have Kérastase or Frédéric Fekkai, that's okay. Buy it. But you don't have to use it every day. In fact, you shouldn't. After a while, your hair gets used to the shampoo and becomes less responsive. So take a week off from the expensive stuff and try a cheaper brand.
- *Downgrade your cuts and colors.* There are plenty of beauty schools that will offer free or discounted haircuts. You're taking a bit of a chance here because it is a cut from someone still in training. But I did it once, and I was pleasantly surprised. Some salons will do this too, especially if they want to try new dyes. Call reputable salons in your area and ask if they need any color models. And maybe you don't need a haircut once a month. Every six weeks could be adequate depending on your hair type.

Baby Got... Great Skin

If you've got bad skin, it doesn't matter if you're wearing a Diane Von Furstenberg wrap dress, a Tom Ford suit, or a track suit. People will notice your skin. So you must take care of it, and you've got to start early. There is a lot

that men and women can do in their twenties to prevent
bad breakouts in their thirties, and it doesn't have to cost
much.

- *Start early.* There are four essentials: cleanser, sunscreen, night cream, and eye cream. If you get into a
  skin care routine in your twenties, it'll spare you the
  cost of antiaging products later on in life.
- *Start cheap and spend more later.* Vander Kolk, the
  director of plastic surgery at Johns Hopkins, said
  a good cleanser and moisturizer twice a day is
  essential. When you're young, go with basic over-
  the-counter products such as Aveeno. Your skin will
  change as you get older. Presumably, you will have
  more disposable income by then. If that's the case,
  he said, get a prescription for Retin-A, an antiaging
  solution.
- *Try baby oil.* Raquel Vincent, a twentysomething in
  New York City who blogs about fashion and beauty,
  said her trick is Johnson & Johnson's Baby Oil Gel.
  Keep it in the shower. After washing with a moisturizing body wash, smooth the oil onto your arms,
  paying particular attention to your elbows and legs.
  Rinse it off as you continue to rub it in. After your
  shower, dry off and apply a daily moisturizing lotion.
  Or just pat dry.

Makeup: To Skimp or Not to Skimp

There are so many brands out there at so many prices.
Should you go for that Chanel nail polish or can you settle

for Revlon? Feel free to go for the cheaper nail polish, mascara, lip gloss, and blush, two beauty experts I asked said. But when it comes to these items, you might want to invest in the good stuff.

- *Concealer:* This will help with dark circles under your eyes. It will also hide a blemish. Use a brush. You use less when you do.
- *Foundation:* This is the base of your makeup, so you don't want to go wrong. Ask the salesperson at the makeup counter for tips. But make sure she does not work on commission. If she does, she'll probably push the most expensive products.
- *Powder:* This will keep your makeup from wearing off. You will use less if you apply it with a washable puff.

Home Runs

A number of beauty experts advocate making your own beauty creams, facial masks, moisturizers, hair treatments. They raid their refrigerators and kitchen cupboards for ingredients such as avocados, strawberries, yogurt, sour cream, honey, and baking soda.

"You can remove your makeup with Crisco or department store cream," said Janice Fox, a well-known proponent of the do-it-yourself beauty product movement and author of *Natural Beauty at Home.* "They are both similar but it's just how you're going to feel about yourself. There are just people who feel if they spend more, they feel better."

Here are some easy recipes Fox had to offer:

- To keep your feet soft, add one cup of white vinegar to a tub of water and soak for fifteen to twenty minutes before giving yourself a complete pedicure. The acid in the vinegar softens and removes rough skin.
- To treat dry, damaged hair, use pure honey as a hair conditioning pack. Massage a tablespoon or two into damp hair and let it sit for fifteen to twenty minutes. Rinse with warm water.
- Use green tea as a toner for your skin, especially for troubled or blemished skin. Spray or apply with a clean cotton pad after cleansing. There is no need to rinse.
- Instead of an expensive night cream, use a rich natural oil such as coconut, almond, or macadamia nut oil. You can also dab some vitamin E oil under your eyes.

Chapter Epilogue

Remember the $445 I dropped on Orlane products in Chicago? When I returned to DC, I drove to Neiman Marcus and returned them. The saleswoman behind the counter shot me a look of disgust, but I didn't care. I couldn't justify the expense after my parents had lent me money.

A few months later, in October, after my planner put me on a budget, I had another victory, albeit a much smaller one. I had been coveting Kérastase shampoo for months after trying it once while staying with my friend Ilana in New York. She has great hair. I too had great hair after using her Kérastase. I spotted it at an Aveda salon in DC as my colleague and good friend Amit and I walked around Dupont Circle.

"No, that is not in your budget," Amit said. A bottle was $32.

The saleslady, overhearing our conversation, grabbed a bottle of Aveda shampoo. "It sounds like this is more in your price range," she said.

It was $9.50.

"You're allowed," Amit, my voice of reason, declared. But even then, I felt guilty about buying it when I had a bottle of Herbal Essences in my bathtub.

"No, I'll just finish my Herbal Essences," I said.

ten
the price of fun

One of the benefits of living with your significant other is that you don't spend as much money on social activities. With both my live-in boyfriends, I much preferred cooking or ordering food and having a bottle of wine in the comfort of our home.

When I became single in July 2005, and then again in April 2007, I started going out almost every night because I didn't want to stay home alone. I was afraid if I did I would watch *The Way We Were* or listen to Sinead O'Connor's "Nothing Compares 2 U" over and over again and cry for hours. To be honest, I did do that on a few nights, and a few nights was about all I could handle.

Once I started getting over the second heartbreak, I actually liked being out on the social scene again. I reconnected with old friends and made new ones. I started throwing more parties and gathering groups of people at various bars and restaurants. Fancy Nancy, which is what some of my friends call me, was back.

Unfortunately, being a gal about town costs money.

Soon after I became a personal finance writer, I decided to write a story about how people my age spend so much money on fun in DC, which often lands near the top of lists ranking cities by how expensive they are. Curious to see if there were others like me, I asked three people to spend two weeks in late 2007 keeping track of how much they were spending on fun. Meetings planner Paxton Styles, graphic designer William Murray, and public relations director Linda Dickerhoof were all exactly my age, single, and childless.

When I first met him, Paxton liked clubbing with friends and drinking Crown Royal whiskey. Such expensive taste in beverages had quite an impact on his bank account. In two weeks, he spent $680.43 on his social life. Much of that—$296.16—went toward bar and nightclub tabs. Happy hours cost him $133. Dinners and late-night munching to soak up the booze were another $94.92.

Paxton was easily going out four or five times a week, which means that a good chunk of the $47,000 a year he was earning was going toward having fun.

"I spend too much money on the partying," Paxton acknowledged over coffee one afternoon.

It's a familiar refrain among people my age living in urban areas. You spend your days in front of a computer dealing with demanding bosses. You walk out of the office, and there's always something to do, someone to see, something to drink, some new restaurant to try. What's wrong with partying hard after working so hard?

Here's what's wrong. You probably can't afford it. You're probably making a decent income but not as good as it will be when you're older and more experienced. You probably think retirement is so far off that you don't really need to get serious about saving yet. You probably put everything on a credit or debit card, so you're not really paying attention to how much your fun is costing you.

Here's how much fun costs: According to Zagat's customer-ranked 2008 restaurant guide, the average cost of a meal for one person is $33.42 nationwide. My city is above the national average at $34.69. In 2007, the average U.S. movie ticket was $6.88, up from $4.59 a decade earlier. At Pacific's the Grove Stadium 14 movie theater in Los Angeles, one adult ticket costs $10.75. An orchestra seat for *Mamma Mia!* on Broadway is about $145. The Champagne Desire cocktail at Blackbird restaurant in Chicago is $12.

"We work so hard in building our careers," said Keva Sturdevant, a financial advisor for Merrill Lynch. "The younger generation wants to see that immediate reward for their hard work, so they spend and hang out with friends and shop. I'm not saying you shouldn't do that, but there should be limits based on your particular financial situation."

Limits—that dreadful word. I had obviously not been good at setting them for myself. Part of the reason is the culture of our nation's capital. Networking is both a necessity and a recreational sport in DC. It is a town of lawyers, lobbyists and consultants, power lunches, happy hours, and party-hopping. There are people who make tons of money and people who make so-so money, and you don't want to be shut out of the social scene even if your salary cannot sustain it. "I think sometimes people will spend in order to fit in," said Kim Reed, a financial planner in Chevy Chase, Maryland.

After realizing how much his social life was affecting his finances, Paxton resolved to make some changes. Although he has no car payment, student loans, or credit card debt, he does worry about his future financial stability. He pledged not to drink for a month to see how much money he would save—and how many pounds he would lose.

William too admitted to having a love of good food and potent drinks. He called himself "The Cruise Director."

"On any given night, someone's out," he said while sipping beer at an Arlington, Virginia, bar. "I float freely between social circles, and that definitely adds to my social costs."

William was in pretty good shape financially when I met him. He was making about $90,000 a year, putting what he could in his 401(k), and building up his savings. His rent was $1,000 and his car payment was $400 a month.

During his first week tracking expenses, he spent $201.30 on dinners and drinks with friends. There was the $14 pitcher of beer at a bar, $29.56 on a birthday dinner, and $16.14 for snacks to watch a football game at a friend's house. He spent quite a bit on himself, too, buying a $659.34 Xbox 360 Elite bundle with *Guitar Hero II* and *Halo 3*. He spent $154.38 on fun during the second week.

Like me, he had another expensive hobby—traveling. He paid about $4,600 for a cruise on the *Queen Victoria* for himself and his brother. Yes, he acknowledged, if he cut back on trips he would probably own a house by now. But he'd rather see the world than own a home. That's the trade-off he's chosen to make.

Trade-offs—a word many people don't like to hear, especially Linda. That's what her life has been about since she bought a two-bedroom duplex in South Arlington, Virginia.

When she participated in this experiment, she was making about $70,000 a year. Her monthly mortgage payment was $1,600. She had about $10,000 in credit card debt and each month paid $300 in student loans, $400 for her car, and $150 for insurance.

"It's very easy for me to get $100 out of the ATM machine. The next thing you know, I'm buying a coffee, I'm buying this and that, and it's gone," she said.

There was the $89.04 Halloween costume. She was a vampire. The cover charge for the party she went to at a restaurant in downtown DC was $10. Beer cost $20. When she ran out of cash, she put $11 on her credit card.

One Friday night, she went to a hockey game at the Verizon Center. The ticket was $35. She arrived at the game with $60 in cash. That disappeared after paying for parking for her designated driver, having pregame beers, beers at the Verizon Center, then postgame beers.

"I own a house now. I have a dog who requires dog food and stuff....I have so many different responsibilities, and I can't go out and spend a couple of hundred dollars on a lunch tab," she said.

More than a year after this experiment, I checked back with Paxton, William, and Linda. Paxton didn't completely give up drinking, but he did stop going out during the week and saved a lot of money. He began cooking at home more often and eating leftovers for lunch. He stopped using his credit cards and stuck to a budget.

William had gotten a raise, but then his company froze salaries and suspended contributions to employees' 401(k)s because of the economic downturn. That forced him to reassess his finances even more. Thankfully, he started dating someone who enjoys cooking at home with him. Instead of taking three big trips a year, he plans to take one. And he's picking up freelance assignments to supplement his income.

Linda got a new, higher-paying job in public relations and signed up to teach a community college class. Next, she created a budget and began dining at home more often. The money she saved she began stashing away in a "secret" credit union account that she can access only in person. She has no debit card linked to it, no checks, and no online access. That cuts down on the temptation to withdraw the money.

I managed to help Paxton, William, and Linda get their arms around their spending. Now it was my turn.

Check, Please

I keep all my receipts. That's a good thing. But I don't keep them in an orderly fashion. That's a bad thing. I have receipts everywhere—on my desk at home, in a cabinet next to my front door, in my nightstand, in my bookshelves, in a kitchen drawer, in my desk at work.

One Saturday afternoon in September 2008, I walked around my apartment scooping them up. Some were crumpled up, some were folded. It was all too much. I wasn't going to figure out how much I spend this way. I came up with a better idea. I got online and checked the summaries for the two bank accounts I keep. I use my debit cards for a lot, so this method would provide me a good snapshot of my spending.

I checked Citibank first. The balance was $549.06. Yikes. I went through every line item.

- *September 15, 2008:* $117 for drinks and dinner for three at Bar Pilar, one of my favorite spots. I put the whole bill on my card and took my friends' cash. My portion of the check was $30. It had been a long day of work, writing about the financial crisis. Wall Street icon Lehman Brothers declared bankruptcy. Merill Lynch sold itself to Bank of America in desperation. Insurance giant AIG had just been rescued by the federal government. The financial world was imploding, and I was on my eighth straight day of working. I needed a drink—or two, and I was hungry.
- *September 9*: $51.20 for a few bottles of wine at the Whole Foods grocery store to take to various parties I was planning to attend.
- *September 5*: $16.30 for a couple of drinks at a birthday party at the Beacon Bar and Grill, an establishment near work.
- *August 31*: $17.29 for lunch at Tryst, a coffeehouse in my neighborhood. I bought my friend a chai latte.
- *August 29*: $32.10 for drinks and appetizers at the Tabard Inn, an upscale restaurant (and I didn't even get an entrée!).

- *August 29*: $151 for a one-way Amtrak ticket from New York back to DC that morning. I had been visiting family.
- *August 23*: $47.05 for dinner and wine at Enology, a new, hip wine bar. It was Saturday. I figured I was allowed.
- *August 18*: $37.08 for drinks for myself and a friend who was celebrating his birthday at the Heights, a new restaurant I had wanted to check out for a while.
- *August 18*: $70, my portion for dinner with three girlfriends at Napoleon, a French bistro I frequent. We split a bottle of wine, each had an entrée, and shared dessert. Then I had a cognac. Yes, we went all out. (And it wasn't even a weekend night!)

My Bank of America balance: $1,288.06. That was a bit of an improvement from my Citibank account.

- *September 13*: $60.85 for bread, pasta salad, and wine for a bridal shower I was cohosting. I had already spent $90 on other items for the shower.
- *September 8*: $34.05 for a couple of glasses of wine at the Tabard Inn. I also pitched in for a friend's part of the bill. It was his birthday.
- *August 28*: $126.20 for drinks and appetizers at the Half King restaurant in Manhattan. I used my card to cover the whole bill, and my two friends gave me cash. My portion was actually $42.
- *August 26*: $103 for a one-way Amtrak ticket to New York.

- *August 22*: $38.40 for lunch for me and a friend to celebrate his birthday. I'm noticing a trend here. I spend a lot on my friends' birthdays.
- *August 18*: $101.75 at a restaurant in New York. I'm assuming the friends I was with pitched in for it, but I can't remember how much.

That was it for the month. But my bank account summary did not give me a complete picture. There were many ATM withdrawals, and much of that money, I'm sure, went toward drinks or my share of dinners. I also did not have a good grasp of how much I spend on transportation. There were times when I could easily have taken the Metro or bus but was running late, as I usually am, and ended up doing the expensive, lazy thing. A cab ride to the neighborhoods I hang out in usually runs about $7 or $8.

I also spend a lot on friends. I can't help it. I cherish my friends and I grew up with a generous mother. The very few times she went out to restaurants, she would often insist on paying for her companions. Another problem: I was splurging on nights when I really didn't need to. Dinner with a friend never seemed to happen at a dive bar.

Must I Shun Fun?

It's okay to spend on your social life, but you have to consider how much you make, how much debt you carry, and how high your monthly fixed costs are, my planner said. If you don't have many expenses, you can spend more on fun. If you are living paycheck to paycheck, it's the first thing you should cut out. It's that simple.

Okay, it's not. But you don't have to shun the fun. Just scale back. Here are some ideas I, and some financial advisors I talked to, came up with:

- When you hit a bar, buy two drinks instead of four. It'll be better for your liver and your calorie count.
- Go to a matinee instead of an evening showing of a movie, or wait for it to come out on DVD. If you have cable, you can get plenty of great movies On Demand for less than a movie ticket. Or if you've got premium channels, you can order the movies being shown that month for free.
- Be picky about the concerts you go to. Now, there are some bands that you will simply have to see live if they show up in your town. For me, a U2 or Radiohead concert is nonnegotiable. But others, you can probably do without.
- You can eat at nice restaurants, but do it only on special occasions or a few times a month.
- Rather than meeting a friend for dinner, eat at home and meet for a drink or coffee.
- If you do have dinner with your friend at a restaurant, share two appetizers and one entrée. If you're like me, you can't finish an entire dish by yourself.
- Become a regular at some nightspots and get to know the bartenders and/or owners. They'll usually slip you a free drink or give you a discount.
- Entertain at home, and ask your friends to bring dishes or drinks. My closest friends in DC all live

within five blocks from me. We call ourselves the Ontario Road crew because we have either lived in, live in, or frequently visit a small apartment building on that street. About once a week, we get together at someone's house for what we've called our family dinner. During the summer, we barbecue. During the winter, we do Taco Tuesday or other theme nights. It's so much better than going to a noisy restaurant. And it provides all sorts of fodder for laughter. You get to make fun of the person who clearly doesn't know how to dice tomatoes. (That person tends to be me.)

Traveling on a Budget

Traveling is great fun but can put a big dent in your budget. My brother-in-law works for two airlines and can sometimes get me buddy passes that require me to pay only taxes and fees. But that only works for last-minute traveling. And sometimes, tickets on popular flights are not available. If I really have to be somewhere on a certain date, I'll use my frequent-flier miles. I book way in advance because those seats tend to disappear quickly.

If I can't use miles, I check online. There's no shortage of websites with deals on hotel rooms, car rentals, and airfare. A few to look at are Expedia.com, Orbitz.com, Travelocity .com, Sidestep.com, Kayak.com, and Priceline.com.

However, you can't completely ignore the airline websites. Many are trying to steer people away from the third-party sites and back to their own. Increasingly, they are giving out promotional codes or e-mailing newsletters with discounts, especially on last-minute travel, to their frequent fliers. Beware of restrictions, though.

Also, don't be afraid to negotiate with the airline. A lot of airlines offer low-fare guarantees now. My friend Elham recently found the same American Airlines flight for less on Expedia. She bought the ticket on American's website, copied and pasted screenshots of Expedia's page with the flight and price information, and sent it to American's low-fare guarantee department. She got a $100 promotion code ($50 for each of two tickets she bought) that she can apply to her next purchase.

When it comes to accommodations, you don't always have to pay for a hotel. Elham discovered HomeExchange .com when researching a trip to Napa Valley or Sonoma for her and her husband. She paid $79.99 for a year's membership (it had been $99.99 but she got a 20 percent discount code at KnowYourTrade.com, a home exchange directory). She listed their gorgeous Adams Morgan townhouse and named their desired travel destinations. She immediately got e-mails from people expressing interest in her home. There are properties all over the world that she is eyeing.

Daphne scopes out Craigslist in the city she is visiting. Many people rent their apartments for much less than a hotel would cost.

If you opt for a hotel, see if they'll give you a free night or other discount. Some of the smaller chains are willing to do so if you tell them you have your eye on another place.

A Few Words on Entertaining at Home

My friend Amit wanted to cook a Sunday roast one weekend after I had started seeing my planner. When the
butcher at Whole Foods said our five-pound roast would
cost us about $80, I turned to Amit and asked: "Why can't
we just make chicken?" The whole point of cooking at
home was to save money. He insisted on the roast and
paid for it. It was a fantastic dinner, but not one I could
afford on my own.

Another friend, Christina Davidson, has perfected the
art of throwing dinner parties on a budget. She and a
small group of friends have dubbed themselves "frugali-
cious foodies." So many of their guests asked for their
recipes that they started a blog called Feedthemasses.org.
In exchange for sharing their secrets, they ask that their
friends donate to a charity or food bank.

Their biggest secret is this: They don't have recipes.
They have principles. Christina said I could share them:

1. *Burn your cookbooks.* Don't look at a recipe and
   create a shopping list of items you won't use again.
   There's probably a lot you can do with what you
   already have in your fridge. Or with what you can
   get on sale at your local grocery store.
2. *Stock your kitchen:* Keep your basic cooking supplies around: Olive oil, vegetable oil, balsamic
   vinegar, honey, flour, brown sugar, eggs, canned
   tomatoes, frozen vegetables, garlic, olives, beans,
   pasta, and rice. You can get a lot of these supplies

for much less at ethnic grocery stores. A tiny bottle of curry powder that is $4 at the supermarket is $6.99 a pound at the Indian grocery store. Pick up some pine nuts and chili paste at the Korean market, some chorizo at the Mexican bodega, and some goat from the Pakistani halal butcher.

3. *Stop wasting perfectly good food.* Christina was at a party a while ago and saw some moldy strawberries. When she tried to toss them, the host intervened. He lectured her, while taking bites of the nonmoldy parts of the strawberry, about how American consumer culture has instilled a fear of any food item that looks less than perfectly fresh. I spent Election Night 2008 with Christina and had delicious banana bread made from overripe bananas while watching the returns. Remember, Christina said, you can freeze food. Peel it, chop it, grate it, or dice it, stick it in a bag and toss it in the freezer.

4. *Grow and make your own.* Save the bones and make your own chicken or beef stock, which generally costs $3 for 32 ounces. Christina said she makes a 10-quart pot of stock for less than $3 in ingredients. Even though she lives in a small apartment in DC, she grows her own herbs outside her windowsill. Think about how much a small package of herbs generally costs. Christina also makes her own salad dressings, marinades, hummus, and other sauces. "You just have to use a little creativity and imagination," she said.

Spending Less Money? Now That's Fun

I was determined to have fun even on a budget. I have to admit, my results in the fall and winter of 2008 were mixed.

I spent the last weekend of November in New York. On November 30, I planned to have brunch with Michael Luo, a *New York Times* reporter whom I had worked with at the *Los Angeles Times* years ago. He and his wife picked BLT Market. When he told me it was at the Ritz-Carlton, I should have had him suggest another place. But I didn't.

It was a prix-fixe brunch. For $38, I got an entrée and a sparkling wine. I asked for a latte and the bagel and lox platter. It came with cream cheese and capers. I had asked them to hold the onions. The plate showed up with no onions and no tomato, I like my lox and bagel with a couple of slices of tomato, so I called the waiter over and asked for some. It took several minutes for him to deliver a small plate with about six tomato slices. I used two. Later when the bill arrived, I noticed that the latte was $7. And there was an $8 charge for the tomatoes: I was shocked. Perhaps, they could have not charged me for the tomato slices given that I asked them to hold the onions? My portion of the bill came to $60.

The next day, the National Bureau of Economic Research, the entity charged with officially declaring recessions, did so. It was my last day in New York. My longtime friend and traveling partner Roy and I have a tradition. We go to Shun Lee Palace East near Penn Station for Peking Duck before I get on the train to DC. Roy wanted the full duck.

"We're in a recession," I snapped. "We can't have a full duck."

"A full duck is better than a half duck," he said.

He asked for the full duck and took the leftovers home. It was a $65-a-person meal with an appetizer, the full duck, some rice, and wine. I clearly had to get out of New York at that point.

I was much more successful the following week. On December 8, Daphne and I met up for dinner before going to our friend's rock band's concert. We were exhausted but had promised to act as groupies for the band. Neither one of us wanted to drink alcohol either. We went to an Ethiopian restaurant and had Diet Cokes and a bunch of meat and veggie dishes. It's amazing how much you save when you don't order alcohol. We each paid $20. I went home early and watched *Miracle on 34th Street*.

Four days later, I accepted my other good friend Jennifer's invitation to dinner and a movie at her house. She had leftover homemade macaroni and cheese. She's a great cook, so I was happy to have the leftovers. While I was still at work, she called and said she wanted to order Chinese food instead.

"My financial planner would really want me to have the mac and cheese," I told her.

"Order Chinese for yourself," I said. "I'll take the leftovers." They were very satisfying, and Jennifer gave me one of her fortune cookies.

It was the best fortune I had ever gotten: "You should be able to make money and hold on to it."

eleven
hot wheels

When I graduated from Georgetown in 1998, my parents gave me the most practical gift they could, considering that I was moving to Los Angeles that fall. It was a brand new Mazda Protégé, a modest and reliable vehicle.

I had just gotten my driver's license and was too afraid to drive the car. Having grown up in New York City, I either walked or took the subway everywhere. Even if we needed a car, my father probably wouldn't have taught me to drive anyway. He taught my brother but didn't bother with my mom, sister, or me. He was a bit conservative and believed that men had their traditional roles. Women had theirs. And in his mind, the only people in our family who needed to drive were the men. He later realized what an error that was.

When the *Post* hired me as a summer intern, I rejoiced until an editor called to tell me: "We really think you should learn how to drive."

I enrolled in the first driving school listed in the phone book. A few times a week, a tiny fifty-something-year-old woman named Lottie would show up at my group house in Georgetown in a banged-up Ford Escort. Lottie always had a bag of barbecue Fritos to snack on while I drove. Lottie did what she could in the little time we had before my internship was to begin. We covered parallel parking in one lesson, but we didn't get to U-turns. I somehow passed the driver's exam, which I joke had more to do with my connection to Lottie than my skills. When the testing administrators at the DC DMV spotted her the day of my exam, they smiled and, almost in unison, exclaimed "Lottie!" She sashayed up to them, hugged them, and said: "I've got another one for you."

After a year learning the rough roads of LA—and considering that switching lanes was one of my biggest fears, it truly was rough—I returned to the *Post*. I drove the car to and from my Maryland satellite office every weekday for years. I drove it up and down the New Jersey Turnpike countless times to visit my parents. I drove it to and from Annapolis and Baltimore for outings with friends. I logged almost 130,000 miles in that car, and it looked it. My friends nicknamed it the Dimpled Trejos because it had so many nicks and dents. I once had to get a new bumper because I drove the car into a pillar while trying to park it in my office building's garage.

The summer before I turned thirty, in 2006, I had had enough of the Dimpled Trejos. It all started when the air-conditioning broke down. I took it to a mechanic who told me it would cost something like $1,500 to fix. Somehow I convinced myself that it made more sense to buy a new car that I wouldn't have to constantly repair than it would to fix my old one. I decided that a woman my age needed to have a decent-looking car. I chose a Volkswagen Beetle simply because I loved playing the Punch Buggy game when I was a kid. My friends and I would run around Queens searching for Bugs and punching each other when we found one (Punch Buggy Yellow! we would shout with glee midpunch.) After weeks of sweating in the Dimpled Trejos, I pulled up to a Volkswagen dealership in Maryland all by myself and, in less than an hour, picked out a 2001 silver Beetle with about 42,000 miles. No research, very little negotiating, nothing. With no money for a down payment, I secured a five-year loan for the entire amount—about $12,000—at an interest rate of almost 10 percent. My credit card debt seemed manageable at the time. For some reason, I figured I could afford an extra $300 a month in payments on top of $100 in insurance.

Less than a year later, I was transferred to our downtown newsroom and no longer needed a car because I could take the bus to work. By that point, the $400 a month had become a nuisance. I tried selling it on Craigslist but soon came to realize there was no way I would be able to get anyone to pay me enough to cover the loan.

I was, as they say in banking parlance, upside down on my car loan.

My car was the second major purchase I had made thus far in my life. Just like I had done with the condo, I had woefully screwed it up. That's what you get for not even checking the Kelley Blue Book value before buying a car. I had not done my due diligence, and I paid for it.

"I frequently tell my clients that car loans are some of the most dangerous loans because they so often trap you," said Mark Jones, a credit counselor and car loan expert at

Credit Counseling of Arkansas. "People come in and it's a $500–$600 a month debt. Now it's such a burden they have to let the loan go bad. With a mortgage, most of the time if you get in trouble you can sell the house. Car debt will always trap you unless you put a lot of money down or you're buying a used vehicle."

In the era of easy credit, people didn't have to come up with down payments to buy cars. When it came to auto loans, consumers applied the same logic they did to mortgages. The more nontraditional loan you could get, the more car you could buy. A decade ago, it was rare for auto loans to last longer than five years. Now, many people have loans that go for seven or eight. Such arrangements were attractive because they didn't require down payments and lowered monthly payments, but they also significantly increased the amount of interest the borrower paid.

They also upped the likelihood that a borrower would default on the loan. This is already happening with more frequency. In 2009, auto loan delinquencies were expected to hit their highest level in at least seventeen years, according to TransUnion Trend Data, which sampled a database of 27 million anonymous consumer records. More Americans were expected to lose their jobs in 2009, which meant that more would probably also lose their cars.

Ruth Martinez, a twenty-seven-year-old secretary in Maryland, was dangerously close to losing her car when I talked to her as the economy deteriorated in 2008. She had missed two payments. She bought her used Honda Odyssey in 2006 on what she considered good terms. With no down payment, she and her husband, a construction worker, got a $16,000 loan at an 8 percent interest rate. To keep the monthly payment down, they accepted a six-year loan. But they were trying to do too much with the $50,000 they made each year. Martinez tapped her credit card to pay for utilities and groceries. Eventually, she racked up $5,000 in credit card debt. Rent was $1,335 a month. The day-care bills for their two children were mounting. And the couple owed $400 to Bank of America each month for their car.

"It's just so stressful," Martinez said. "To be young and to have a family going through this, it's hard."

There was not much Martinez and her husband could do but explain their situation to the bank and plead for leniency.

"It's a very difficult problem to solve once you're there," Jones said.

The key is to try to keep yourself from getting there. I wanted to understand what I did wrong, so I asked several experts to explain to me how you should buy a car.

Shop Around

First, ask yourself if you really need a car. If you decide you do, the best scenario is to save for it and pay for it outright in cash. I know that many of you, like me, don't have that much cash lying around, in which case, you will have to shop for a loan.

This will be tricky. Banks have been holding on to their money a lot more tightly in this recession. If your credit is not stellar, you might want to consider holding off until you clean it up.

If your credit is good enough, you have to figure out how much you can afford to pay. Don't just think about the purchase price. Factor in the other costs of owning a vehicle—insurance, maintenance, registration, gasoline, parking. Make sure you have money set aside for regular upkeep and unscheduled repairs.

Consider getting preapproved for a loan so you have a better idea of what you can buy. If you don't have at least 20 percent to contribute as a down payment, you're probably going to end up paying a higher interest rate.

Once you have figured out your budget, you're probably going to ask yourself: Should I buy new or used?

Many buyers go for new cars because presumably, if well-built, they won't require repairs for a while, and if they do, they come with warranties. Keep in mind, though, that you can find used cars that are reliable and in good condition if they were well-maintained by the previous owner. Many used cars also still have warranties.

I don't want to burst your bubble if your dream has always been to buy yourself a shiny new BMW for your thirtieth birthday, but many experts argue that a used car is the way to go. The average new car depreciates by 50 percent in the first four years. Used cars don't have as far to fall in value.

"Cars are money pits and they depreciate rapidly," said Frank Boucher, the Virginia financial planner. "Today's cars are made to last many years without the maintenance that they used to require. You can save a ton of money by buying used and you can buy a can of spray for that new car smell."

Once you've settled that matter, it's time to decide on a vehicle. You won't have a difficult time gathering information about any type of car you're considering. Read advice columns and consumer reports online or in newspapers. Compare prices. If you're buying a used car, check the Kelley Blue Book value. Research your choice on other websites such as Edmunds.com.

Arm yourself with as much information as you can before you call up that owner advertising on Craigslist or hit the car dealership. Be prepared to ask a lot of questions, and don't be afraid to negotiate.

Try not to go to the car dealership alone, like I did. Take a parent or trusted friend. Don't fall for any gimmicks or fancy advertisements, of which there will be many. Ignore those low-payment, low-interest, bad credit–no problem ads. And beware of special financing deals, which salespeople often offer instead of rebates. Do the math to figure out which one is the better fit for you financially.

"Don't be afraid to shop around and don't cave to high pressure," Boucher said. "Of course the salesman is nice. He's trained to be nice. That's how he sells cars."

Don't go soft on him just because he smiles a lot. If he doesn't agree to your price, walk away and stay away. You'd be surprised. If the salesperson has had a slow month and is not going to meet his quota, he might end up calling you back.

Once you've agreed to buy a car, the salesperson will escort you to the financing and insurance person. That person will try to sell you everything—extended warranties, security systems, you name it. You should think about this ahead of time and know what you want before you walk into that dealership.

"I was sold a special security system for $300, which I have never used and the cost was rolled into my loan," Boucher said. "That was really stupid. What's worse, it broke after a couple of years."

I too was sold an extended warranty and a number of other things I can't even remember now. Had I done my research, or had I been accompanied by someone who knew something about cars, I would have said no to that friendly financing guy.

If it's a used car, make sure you have it inspected. If you are buying it from a private owner, be sure to get the vehicle identification number (VIN) and run a vehicle history report from CARFAX or AutoCheck. You should be able to find out if the car has been involved in an accident or a theft.

Remember, you can negotiate with individual owners as well. In fact, you will probably get a better price from private sellers, many of whom are in predicaments like mine. I tried to sell my car on Craigslist for $10,000. I got an e-mail from an interested buyer.

"Will you go below $10,000?" he asked.

"No," I said.

"You're asking too much," he wrote, pointing out that my asking price was above the Blue Book value. (The last time I checked, I could expect $5,980 for it as a private seller. A dealer could get $7,980 if it were in excellent condition.)

Perhaps I should have sold him the car, but at the time

it seemed I would be taking too much of a hit. He never tried to negotiate with me. I'm sure he had plenty of other options, especially now that both dealers and individual owners are trying to unload their cars.

Start Your Engines

Once you settle on a car, you'll have to get your financing in order. Just as you shopped around for the car, shop around for the loan. Financing a car through the dealer is an option, but it will probably cost you more than if you go with your credit union or bank. Whatever you do, don't fall for the low monthly payment, seven-year loan trap. Try to get a loan for the shortest duration possible. You don't want the loan to outlast the car. And ask about any rebates.

You'll also have to shop around for auto insurance. Check such websites as InsWeb.com or Insurance.com. Your rates will be based on some factors that you can't control— your age, sex, marital status, and place of residence—and others that you can—your credit score, choice of vehicle, driving record, and extent of coverage. If you want a lower rate, keep your credit history clean, don't speed, and think twice before buying a sports car. If you can afford to pay a little more out of pocket, then consider increasing your deductible—or your share of the cost—for comprehensive and collision coverage. Comprehensive coverage covers a theft or any other noncollision damage to your car. A higher deductible will reduce your premium.

Once you have your car, drive it until its wheels fall off. "The least expensive car you will ever own is the car you own now. You cannot go back to a prior car and you will almost always buy a more expensive car when you replace the car you have now," said David Roddick, a certified credit counselor at the Consumer Credit Counseling Service of Forsyth County.

Damaged Goods

Let's say you didn't drive the car until its wheels fell off, only until the air-conditioning broke down and the car was so banged up that it became the butt of all your friends' jokes. Yes, I am talking about myself, but you too might have dumped your car before you had sucked all the life out of it. You too might have replaced it with a car you really could not afford. And you too might now be underwater on your loan. By some estimates, 40 percent of consumers are upside down on their car loans.

If you're in that situation, what are your options?

Until the recession, if you were looking to buy a new car when you were upside down on your old one, lenders were willing to add the remaining balance to the new loan. Not anymore. But there are other options. Automakers often give cash rebates to customers that they can then apply to the purchase of the new car. Increasingly, many of them are letting customers use the rebate to pay off the old loan.

If you're not in the market to buy a new car, you can try to sell your old one to a place like CarMax. The good thing about CarMax is that you can walk in there and get rid of your car in one afternoon. But CarMax may lowball you. I, unfortunately, turned to CarMax just as the economy was getting worse and people stopped buying cars.

It was mid-October 2008. I had not gotten any good offers on Craigslist. For months, I had been driving my car with the passenger side rearview mirror hanging off. I found it that way one morning. I assumed it had been knocked off by a drunk person returning from one of the bars in my neighborhood. I knew it could not have been a hit-and-run because the car was parked with the passenger side against the curb. A friend had tried to patch it up with black tape. I left it that way for fear that it would cost too much to repair. Someone suggested I get my insurance company to cover it. I called and got it declared an act of vandalism. State Farm gave me the number for a glass company, and I scheduled the repair. I drove it to DC's junkyard city, getting completely lost. It took up most of my workday but my deductible was just $100, which was totally manageable.

Off to CarMax I went. After some polite chitchat, the jolly old guy who inspected my Bug (he did look pretty jolly—big belly, rosy cheeks and all) offered me $4,000.

"It's a tough market," he said. "The credit crunch is making things difficult for everyone."

I had tried to sell it to CarMax once before, about a year before this latest attempt. They offered me $7,500 back then. This is what I get for waiting a year.

I called up my car lender, HSBC, and was told that my payoff quote was slightly more than $10,000.

I drove home and mulled it over. The next day, as I walked to work, I called my parents. My dad was outraged. "They're trying to rob you," he shouted loudly into the phone.

"Please don't yell at me," I said. He wasn't yelling at me, per se. He was just so incensed that he was yelling at the only person he could yell at.

"Don't do it. Just keep the car," he counseled me.

I took his advice—for now.

I could have taken the loss. But I didn't even have enough cash to make up the difference. I could have raided my 401(k) or put it on a low-interest credit card, but my planner Christine counseled against this. Alternately, I could have seen if my employers' credit union, another bank, or even HSBC would give me an unsecured loan for the amount that I owed.

I was reluctant to do this because a $6,000 loan is substantial. I would be making payments, for quite a while, on a car I no longer owned.

Christine checked some websites and saw 2001 Beetles selling for more than the $4,000 CarMax offered me. Her advice was to keep paying my loan down and trying to sell the car until I got a price that wouldn't leave me with a $6,000 deficit.

"I do not think taking a loss would be in your best interest because you would still need to make the payments for the loan," she said. "The title would not clear until then."

Perhaps a $2,000, or even a $3,000, gap would be tolerable. The numbers could work out in the end if I factored in insurance and maintenance costs. Right now, I pay about $1,200 a year in insurance. Even if I had to come up with $2,000 or $3,000 to pay off the bank, I would be saving on all those other costs. But I had to get a better price for it. Back to Craigslist I would have to go, Christine said.

Perhaps someone else who had played the Punch Buggy game will eventually come along. Once I get the Bug out of the way, I will never again buy a car unless I desperately need one. A car is not an investment. It's an expense. What's the point of having a car if you can't afford to buy dinner at the restaurant you drive it to?

twelve
good debt, bad debt

think about my credit card debt all the time. It stresses me out to the point where I can't sleep sometimes. But I hardly ever think of my student loan debt. Each month, Sallie Mae automatically pulls $98 from my bank account. I barely notice it.

I've divided my loans into two categories: Good debt and bad debt.

A bad debt is one you take on for something that declines in value—a depreciating asset, in financial lingo. When you factor in the interest, you are paying a lot more than the original price. My credit card debt would certainly fall under that.

A good debt is one in which the return on the investment is expected to exceed the cost of borrowing. The interest rate is generally low and you're getting something for your money. A mortgage—that is, a thirty-year fixed-rate rather than an exotic adjustable-rate loan—falls under the good debt category. So does a student loan because a college education is a sound investment that increases your earning potential and makes it more likely that you will enjoy employer-provided health care and retirement benefits.

Sometimes, though, good debt can go bad, as I know full well.

Take student loans. Tuitions are soaring across the country, forcing students to borrow more money. They graduate with tens of thousands of dollars in debt, and in this economy, many are not getting high-paying jobs. Most students have loans that are backed by the federal government, which has become much more aggressive at collecting on that debt over the years. Those students with loans from private lenders—loans that are not backed by the federal government—have their own challenges because they are usually paying a higher interest rate.

Larry Glazer, managing partner at Mayflower Advisors in Boston, has a term for these students who find themselves with few hot job prospects and hefty debt at graduation: the Disillusioned Generation. "Their salaries aren't as high as expected and their career path is not what they thought it would be," he said.

And mortgages? Well, we've seen in the last couple of years how easy it is to fall into the trap of overextending yourself to fulfill the American Dream of owning a home.

Perhaps you, like me, are still dealing with your student loans years after graduation. Perhaps you, unlike me, are thinking of buying your first home. Perhaps you are doing both. Whichever you find yourself doing, it's important to figure out how to keep good debt from going bad.

The Price Is Not Always Right

When I went to Georgetown University in the mid-1990s, it cost almost $30,000 a year in tuition, room, board, and fees. Each year, the school gave me about $10,000 to cover part of my costs. My parents contributed a few thousand, and I earned a few thousand more under the federal work-study program. The rest I am still paying off to Sallie Mae in the form of federally guaranteed loans.

You might be asking: Shouldn't I be done by now?

Yes, I should have been done in 2008 if I had stuck with the original plan, which was to pay it off in ten years. But my year of earning a pitiful salary in LA set me back. When I returned to DC, I was hurting financially and asked Sallie Mae to grant me a forbearance, or a temporary suspension of my payments. The interest for that time accrued and was added to the principal of my balance. That increased the total amount I owe. In order to keep my monthly payment low, I also stretched the length of the loan. I have another $12,000 to go.

In retrospect—and in the long-term—this was not the wisest financial move. Over time, it has cost me more money. But my other option was to default, which was certainly not a good move either.

Many graduates are now struggling to keep up with their student loan payments, even on the federally guaranteed ones that have lower interest rates. The U.S. Department of Education, bruised by the high default rates of the early 1990s, is showing no leniency. The agency employs private collection companies to go after seriously delinquent borrowers and can take such actions as garnishing a portion of your wages or confiscating federal and state income tax refunds. Think the agency has forgotten about your unpaid student loan from twenty years ago? Probably not. There's no statute of limitations on unpaid student loans. It has even been known to garnish a portion of your Social Security benefits.

"Anything the government can do to get its money, it will. You don't want to mess with that," said Chris Penn, chief media officer of the Student Loan Network, a lender.

Unlike credit card debt, it's nearly impossible to get student loan debt discharged if you declare bankruptcy. Borrowers have to prove that paying back the loan would cause an "undue hardship."

"A lot is up to the discretion of the judge, and only about half the time people I believe should qualify for an undue hardship discharge are actually granted one," said Mark Kantrowtiz, publisher of FINAID.org, which tracks the student loan industry. "It's a very difficult standard to meet. There's a lot of inconsistency in how it's applied. And these days the lenders are very aggressive in fighting attempts to discharge student loan debt."

There's plenty you can do to keep it from getting to that point, though. First, make sure your lender has your current address. A key reason borrowers default is that they forget about their loans and never tell the lender where to send the monthly bills.

Second, contact your lender before you miss a payment. Lenders are more willing to help borrowers who are still in good standing.

Next, understand what your rights are. What you are eligible for often depends on whether your loan comes directly from the federal government (the Direct Loan Program) or from a private financial institution that has been authorized to issue federally guaranteed loans (the Federal Family Education Loan Program, also known as FFEL). If you can't keep up with your payments, you have two options for suspending them, and they apply to either direct or FFEL loans.

- *Deferment:* You qualify for this if you meet certain conditions, such as being a graduate school student or unemployed or disabled. If you have a Perkins or a subsidized Stafford loan, the federal government continues to pay the interest. (A Perkins loan is awarded to students with an exceptional financial need. A subsidized Stafford loan is one in which the federal government pays the interest while you're in school.) If you have an unsubsidized Stafford loan, you are responsible for paying the interest. You have the option of deferring payment of the interest on unsubsidized loans by capitalizing it (adding it to the amount owed).
- *Forbearance:* If you can't get a deferment, you'll have to settle for the forbearance, which has less favorable terms because the interest will keep accruing, thus increasing the overall size of the loan. You can only do it for twelve-month intervals for up to three years. This is granted at the lender's discretion, usually in cases of financial hardship.

If you don't suspend your payments, you can ask for a longer period of time to repay. The Standard Repayment plan is a fixed monthly amount for a loan term of up to ten years. If you want to shrink your monthly payment, you have options. But remember, the trade-off for the lower monthly payment is that the overall loan size will increase:

- *Extended Repayment:* The loan repayment is spread out over twelve to thirty years to reduce the monthly payment. The length of the repayment term depends on the amount owed.
- *Graduated Repayment:* This plan starts off with a lower monthly payment, then gradually increases it every two years. It lasts between twelve to thirty years. The monthly payment is no less than 50 percent and no more than 150 percent of the payment under the Standard Repayment plan.

These next three are all based on income:

- *Income-Contingent Repayment:* This applies only to Direct Loan borrowers and is based on income and total debt. The monthly payment adjusts every year as the income changes. It can last up to twenty-five years, and any balance left over after that time period is discharged.
- *Income-Sensitive Repayment:* This applies to FFEL loans and lasts only up to ten years. The monthly payments are a percentage of the borrower's gross monthly income.
- *Income-Based Repayment:* Started on July 1, 2009, this applies to both Direct Loan and FFEL borrowers.

It is more generous than the previous two because it caps the monthly payment at a lower percentage of discretionary income. After twenty-five years, any remaining balance is forgiven.

Borrowers should always be on the lookout for loan forgiveness programs from the federal government or their state government.

For instance, there is a public service loan forgiveness program in which the federal government will discharge the remaining debt of borrowers who make 120 loan payments while working full-time in public service jobs. The graduate must be in the Direct Loan program.

Some states, such as Massachusetts, offer their own loan forgiveness programs, so be sure to contact your state higher education organization.

What if you've got a private loan? Private student loans make up about 20 percent of new loans to students. They became so popular because federal aid was not enough to cover the ridiculously high tuitions students were facing. They often have higher rates—about 12 percent (federal loans are now fixed at 6.8 percent). They also come with more fees and prepayment penalties (federal loans do not). These loans have become more scarce during the recession.

If it's too late and you already have a private loan that is overwhelming you, make sure you talk to your lender about your options. Many private lenders will offer deferments, forbearances, or an extended repayment.

The one good thing about the private loans is that the

banks cannot garnish wages without a court order. Still, you want to avoid defaulting because doing so would damage your credit score.

The key to staying out of student loan trouble is to not take on too much debt in the first place. If you're applying for colleges, try to maximize your gift aid. Submit the Free Application for Federal Student Aid to see if you can get a Pell Grant. Search for scholarships on free websites such as FastWeb.com. The more you get in grants and scholarships, the less you'll have to borrow.

I haven't always made the smartest moves with my student loans. Getting a forbearance will cost me more in the long run. It was the right move at the time because it prevented me from defaulting.

There's not much I can do other than continue to repay it on time until I'm done. After all, I have a low interest rate. My financial planner recommended that I pay the minimum required each month, then use any disposable income to wipe out my more expensive debt, particularly my credit cards.

Do I still consider it good debt? I feel that I did get a return on my investment: A job at a newspaper I love.

There's No Place Like Home

The first, and only, home I owned was truly a good debt gone bad. It doesn't have to be that way for you. This is the biggest purchase you will ever make. So please, before you do anything else, ask yourself several questions.

Does it really make sense to buy a home at this stage? If you don't plan on staying for at least five years, it does not. We were spoiled during the real estate boom. Property values rose in a matter of months. That is not how real estate normally works. You will typically have to hold on to a property for at least five years in order to break even or make a profit after you factor in all the costs of buying and owning a home (purchase price plus interest plus insurance plus maintenance plus condo association fees).

Sometimes, it doesn't make sense to buy a home. We've all heard that saying: When you rent, you're throwing away your money. Okay, there is a good point in there. But that doesn't mean renting is automatically a bad thing for some of us. Do the math. Get online and find a rent versus own calculator. They're all over the Internet.

Take Ken Clark, a certified financial planner who writes for About.com. When he lived in California, the home he rented cost him $2,000 a month. To own a comparable home, he calculated that it would cost him $4,500 a month, without even factoring in maintenance. "When there are markets like that when there's such a gap between renting and buying a home, we can excuse not buying a home," he told me.

When he moved to Little Rock, Arkansas, he rented a $2,200 home. A comparable property would cost $2,400 a month to own. It made sense to own under those circumstances. "One of the things we saw in this last economic boom was the feeling of being left out in this real estate market," he said. "Let's make sure it even makes financial sense to own a home before we panic about not owning one."

Do you see a house as a place to live or do you see it primarily as an investment? If it's the latter, you've still got the boom years' mind-set. Too many people stopped seeing their homes as homes and more as piggy banks. The days of flipping properties are over.

Are you comfortable with the responsibilities of owning a home? When you're a renter, if anything goes wrong in your apartment or house, you can call the janitor or the owner to fix it. When you're a home owner, it's up to you. I remember having to get my garbage disposal fixed. I had no idea where to start.

Are you aware of what it costs to be a home owner? The purchase price is just one part of it. You also have to factor in closing costs, which is what you pay when the property is transferred to you. You have to consider the expense of maintaining the home. If you buy a condo, you'll have a monthly condo fee. As a renter, you don't have to pay for things like water. As a home owner, you might. When you sell the place, you'll have more closing costs, which consists of Realtors' fees and taxes, among other things.

• • •

Once you've asked yourself all these questions, check your credit score to make sure you can actually qualify for a mortgage with a low interest rate. Interest rates have been at historic lows the last few years. At one point in early 2009, I had friends scrambling to refinance their mortgages when rates dipped below 5 percent. It was amazing. When my parents bought their first home, their interest rate was in the double digits. But you can't take advantage of these rates if you've got a low credit score. Faced with a wave of foreclosures, banks are scrutinizing new borrowers a lot more.

Next, figure out how much of a down payment you can afford. Again, ideally you would have at least 20 percent of the purchase price. I know that's a lot to ask, especially from a twenty- or thirtysomething. But if you have less than that, you get hit with private mortgage insurance. If you don't have that much in your savings account, financial planners advise getting a gift from a relative. That didn't exactly work out for me, but it is an option for a lot of young people. Although a 20 percent down payment is preferable, a decent option if you don't have that is to get help from the Federal Housing Administration, which has a program that allows borrowers to commit as little as 3.5 percent of the purchase price. Most of the closing costs and fees can be included in the loan. Your state might also have a subsidized mortgage financing program for low- to moderate-income residents. If you're trying to buy a home in your twenties, when you're not making much money, you might qualify.

Also, make sure you keep abreast of tax incentives. For example, President Obama's economic stimulus package included a tax credit for first-time home buyers in 2009 for 10 percent of the home's purchase price up to $8,000.

Now if you have a down payment and a credit score at or above 700, start shopping around for a mortgage. Try multiple lenders. Get preapproved so you know what price range to look at. Only buy what you can afford, not what the bank says you can afford. No more than 25 percent of your pretax income should go toward your mortgage.

Some financial advisors still advocate ARMs if you don't intend to stay in a home for much longer than five years. Others say a thirty-year fixed-rate loan is the way to go. All agree that exotic mortgages, such as 2/28 and 3/27 ARMs with low teaser rates the first two or three years, are out of the question. Actually, you'd have a difficult time finding a bank that still offers them. "The predictability of a thirty-year loan is crucial for a young person whose life might change in a few years," Clark said. "With other mortgages you're playing hot potato with a grenade. As tempting as it is to get more house with one of these mortgages you should not do it."

Now it's time to find a property. Get a good agent. Recommendations from friends help. Interview a few before you settle on one. Decide on a location. Look at crime statistics and the home's proximity to your work. If you are thinking of having children at some point, research the school district and recreational facilities. Also consider the ease of resale. Three- or four-bedroom homes sell better than one- or two-bedroom homes, for instance.

Consider buying a resale yourself. During the real estate boom, developers were quick to build fancy condos and houses in urban and suburban areas throughout the country. Young people in particular were drawn to them. I was. I don't even cook much, yet I insisted on buying a condo with granite kitchen countertops and stainless-steel appliances. "There is greater value in quality, in square footage in older properties. Brand new, they're going to pay top dollar and they're going to be looking at 750 square feet for a one-bedroom," said Melanie Coughlan, a Realtor for Keller Williams Realty in Fairfax and Loudoun Counties, Virginia.

The problem with a lot of those new homes is that they are cookie-cutter. One unit looks just like the one next door. Maybe you can live with that, but when you try to sell it a few years later, you could end up in competition with someone else in your building who has the same product to offer. This happened to me. At one point, there were six other one-bedroom condos for sale in my building. You could barely tell them apart.

If you find a home you like, don't be afraid to offer less than the asking price in this market. Your real estate agent will help you figure out a good offer. Don't forego a home inspection. And ask the seller to pay for all or some of your closing costs.

Worst-Case Scenario

Some of you might already be home owners and on the brink of losing your homes. The White House estimates that about 6 million home owners are facing foreclosure.

When I spoke to Maria Hernandez, twenty-seven, in November 2008, she feared she would lose her suburban Maryland home. She and her husband scrounged together $164,000 for a down payment of more than 20 percent on their four-bedroom colonial. The money came from the profit they made off a smaller house in Virginia plus their savings.

They were supposed to be moving up in the real estate world. Instead, their lives spiraled downward because of a bad mortgage, a bad economy, and a bad housing market. Their mistake: When they bought the house in December 2006, they opted for an adjustable-rate mortgage.

That seemed like a good idea until Rosa lost her job as a receptionist. With just her husband's income as a kitchen manager, they missed a few of their $2,658 monthly payments, even before the interest rate went up. The house, which they bought for $585,000, depreciated to about $400,000.

Rosa had no idea what to do when she wrote me for advice.

The federal government has taken some steps to help home owners like Rosa. On October 1, 2008, federal officials started the Hope for Homeowners program to help borrowers refinance into thirty-year, government-backed mortgages. But banks weren't rushing to participate in the program.

What can Rosa and others like her do in the meantime?

First, they should contact their lender immediately, preferably before they have missed payments.

Diane Cipollone, an attorney and director of Civil Justice's Sustainable Homeownership Project in Baltimore, said they should seek a loan modification, in which the lender changes the terms of the loan. "That will allow them to remain in the home. If their property value increases over time, they may possibly regain some or all of their lost equity," she said.

It is a long and arduous process, and many times, lenders do not consent to it. The problem is that many of the loans were bundled together into mortgage-backed securities and sold off to investors on Wall Street. The lenders cannot modify the mortgages without the consent of all the investors. The investors are not willing to give that consent because they would lose money.

A short refinance is another option, albeit one that is even more out of reach than a modification. It involves another lender agreeing to refinance the loan at the new lower value. Getting the current mortgage company to take less than what is owed is tricky. The current lender itself could also refinance the loan for less than what is owed and forgive the difference.

A similar but less desirable scenario would be a short sale. The lender lets the owner sell the house at a loss and then forgives the debt. But that too is difficult.

One important thing to keep in mind with a short sale or short refinance: You might end up with a big tax bill. Congress temporarily suspended that tax hit in 2008, but consult with a tax attorney or accountant to make sure.

Many community and nonprofit organizations, such as ACORN and NeighborWorks America, are also good resources for endangered home owners. Hope Now is an alliance of counselors, servicers, investors, and other mortgage market participants.

Lastly, Cipollone said, remember this: "All homeowners should ignore solicitations and websites that promise or guarantee to save their homes and should not pay up front for any such promised outcomes."

Make sure any organization you deal with is a nonprofit approved by the U.S. Department of Housing and Urban Development. They are listed on www.hud.gov.

I feel for people in Rosa's situation. For a while, after Live-In Boyfriend #1 and I broke up, I too thought I would not be able to keep up with my mortgage payments. There was no way I could manage $2,100 a month on my own. I may have lost most of the down payment, but at least I wasn't forced out of my home by the bank.

thirteen
sex and the city meets the golden girls

I was at a party in February having a long discussion with an intelligent, successful, twentysomething producer for a major TV news show when, upon learning I was a personal finance writer, she asked me for a bit of advice.

"You know what I just don't get?" she said.

"What?" I asked.

"Saving for retirement. 401(k)s. I just don't get it," she said. "I know what they are but I just don't get it. I know what I have in my bank account. I know how much I have to spend now. But retirement? I have no clue. I can't think that far ahead. A friend of mine said, 'When you're dead you can't spend any money anyway. Why save for it? Why not just enjoy your money now?'"

We all like to picture ourselves wearing Manolo Blahniks and sipping cosmos with our girlfriends every night for the rest of our lives. At some point, though, we're going to have to trade in those stilettos for a comfortable pair of orthopedic shoes and drink tea with our fellow senior citizens at a Florida retirement community. (Maybe it won't be that bad. Maybe we'll be drinking white wine spritzers at the Algonquin Hotel bar in Manhattan wearing sensible heels.)

I know people in their twenties and thirties don't like to think that far ahead, which is why a lot of us don't plan for our retirements. I didn't start a 401(k) until my sixth year at the *Post* even though I was eligible to sign up after my first year. I didn't want to have less take-home pay. In the end, it cost me tens of thousands of dollars in compounded retirement savings. I have also not yet started an IRA, which can have wonderful tax benefits.

Only 48 percent of eligible workers in their twenties contribute to 401(k) plans, according to a 2007 study from consulting firm Hewitt Associates Inc.

Until three decades ago, Social Security and pensions were the main sources of retirement income. Now, Social Security is in danger of running out of money. And pensions, in which employers invest a pot of money and promise to pay employees a set amount each month for the rest of their lives at retirement, are quickly disappearing.

In 1985, there were 29 million participants in pension plans and 10 million in 401(k)s. In 2005, there were 21 million in pension plans and 47 million in 401(k)s. The government has encouraged that shift, providing $80 billion in tax breaks each year to people who stash their money away in 401(k)s. Unlike pensions, 401(k)s and similar vehicles leave the investing up to individual employees even if they know little about the stock market. Also unlike pensions, there is no guarantee that 401(k) money will stretch out over the retiree's lifetime. Whatever employees retire with depends on how well their investments performed.

The dramatic declines in the stock market in the last couple of years have prompted many academics and consumer advocates to question the wisdom of tying so many workers' retirement savings to the whims of the stock market. We could debate this for hours, but the bottom line is twenty- and thirtysomethings cannot count on Social Security or pensions. So we've got to start our 401(k)s early.

"If you truly don't believe Social Security is going to be around and if you don't believe Mom and Dad will leave you an inheritance—statistics show they won't—then you need a pile of money," said Brian Jones, a certified financial planner at CJM Wealth Advisers in Fairfax, Virginia. "That's the basis of retirement planning. The sooner you have your pile of money, the sooner you can retire and do something else."

Financial planners recommend setting aside between 10 to 15 percent of your income in various savings vehicles. In addition to your 401(k)s, you can park your money in IRAs, real estate, or emergency reserve funds.

But first, we've got to understand the difference between tax-deferred and tax-exempt retirement accounts.

With tax-deferred accounts, you contribute a portion of your salary before it is taxed. Whatever income you make from your investments is also not subject to tax while it's in the account. The IRS stays away from all that money until you withdraw it upon retirement. The advantage is that your money will compound more quickly over time than it would if taxes were taken out each year.

With tax-exempt accounts, you contribute a portion of your income after it has already been taxed. But once you retire and withdraw that money, you owe nothing more to the IRS.

Employee-Sponsored Retirement Plans

Most of us know these tax-deferred plans as 401(k)s, but there are other kinds of accounts that fall under this umbrella. For instance, many federal government employees have the Thrift Savings Plan. Employees of nonprofit organizations and certain employees of public schools have the 403(b) plan. They're all similar.

You decide how much of your monthly income to invest in this account. Your employer automatically deducts that from your paycheck. Many employers match a percentage of your contribution—usually 50 cents on the dollar, or even the full dollar, up to 6 percent. There is also a maximum contribution you can make. That changes each year. In 2010, the max is $16,500, or $22,000 if you are fifty and older.

Start as soon as your employer lets you. If you're twenty-five, save $200 a month in a 401(k) that earns an average 10 percent annually (which some would say is an optimistic expectation), then by the time you turn sixty-five, you will have about $1.3 million saved, according to Kiplinger.com. If your employer offers 50 cents of every dollar you contribute, your savings will reach almost $2 million. What if you wait until you are thirty-two? Your savings will be half what you would have earned if you had started seven years earlier, Kiplinger.com said.

Why would you wait? More important, why would you turn down a 401(k) given the tax benefits AND the possible employer match? It's free money.

Choose Your Flavor

These retirement accounts are usually managed by a third-party administrator. Vanguard, Fidelity, and T. Rowe Price are three of the nation's largest 401(k) providers. At the behest of your employer, this third-party administrator will let you pick among several investment types, from the aggressive (stocks) to the conservative (bonds and money market funds).

This is the difficult part. Most young people can't afford financial planners to design for them a good investment portfolio. Your 401(k) provider will ask you to fill out a questionnaire to determine how much risk you can handle without tossing and turning each night. The younger you are, the more risk you should take because your goal is to beat the rate of inflation. Risks beget rewards. Stocks are the riskiest investments. As you get older, you should switch to more conservative investments such as bonds (also known as fixed-income because they provide investors with periodic fixed interest payments).

A good rule of thumb when deciding how much to invest in stocks is to subtract your age from 100. The difference is the percentage of your portfolio to allocate to stocks. For instance, if you are twenty-five years old, you should have 75 percent in stocks. But planners also say you should consider your risk tolerance. If having 75 percent of your portfolio in stocks is going to keep you up at night, perhaps it might be too aggressive.

Whatever you decide, make sure you diversify your portfolio in order to spread that risk. The theory is that if a few of your companies don't do well, others will shine and compensate for it. Put your money in companies of different sizes and in different sectors, such as technology and utilities. Mix in some international investments. You might also be able to buy your own company's stock, but make sure you don't overdo it. (Remember Enron?)

If picking companies to invest in is not your forte—few people know how to do it well and even they make mistakes—then you don't have to worry. Usually, your employer will steer you toward mutual funds, which are pools of investments run by professional managers. More than a quarter of Americans' retirement savings are in mutual funds. Essentially there are three types: equity (stocks), fixed-income (bonds) and money market (which invest mostly in government bonds). Within these categories, there are many flavors. Here are a few that come up frequently:

- *Index Funds:* These baskets of funds try to mirror the performance of a benchmark stock market index such as the Standard & Poor's 500 or the Dow Jones Industrial Average.
- *International Funds:* They invest in companies outside the United States. They carry some risk because you cannot predict an economic or a political crisis in a particular country. But they're great for diversification.
- *Balanced Funds:* Blending stocks and bonds, they tend to be lower risk than stock funds but have a lower potential for return.

- *Specialty Funds:* These concentrate on a segment of the economy, such as technology, health care, and energy. Or they focus on a region of the world. You can also find socially responsible funds investing in companies that are energy-efficient, for example, or shun anything having to do with tobacco.

Invest in three to five different funds at the minimum. Don't go beyond ten. And consider target-date funds, which invest in a mix of stocks, bonds, and money funds based on when you plan to retire. The closer to retirement you get, the more conservative the investments become.

Once you've picked your investments, don't let them get stale. It's important to review your choices each year. Perhaps you'll decide you don't have enough in small-cap growth funds (they invest in small but fast-growing companies). Or you might decide you want more socially responsible companies in your portfolio. Rebalance if necessary—but no more than once a year.

I know many of you are watching or reading the news every day and worrying about losing money in the stock market. I've gotten e-mails from people just starting their first jobs and wondering if they should even bother with a 401(k). If you already have a 401(k), you're probably thinking you should pull your money out. Don't. The worst thing you can do is make an emotional decision. That's how people lose money. The best thing you can do is ride it out. The stock market has always recovered over time. And time is something you have plenty of if you are a twenty- or thirtysomething. When you retire in forty or fifty years, you will almost surely have recovered your savings and then some.

Raiding Your Retirement Piggy Bank

Yes, it's possible to do this, but any planner will tell you: Don't, unless you're on the verge of bankruptcy or fore-closure or need to pay for treatment for a life-threatening illness.

Most, but not all employers, allow you to tap into your nest egg under certain circumstances.

First, there's the hardship withdrawal. This requires proof of a severe immediate, financial need. The IRS has a list of approved reasons, such as medical expenses that insurance won't cover, payments to avoid eviction or fore-closure, funeral expenses, and college tuition. You can also withdraw money for a down payment toward a house.

But hardship withdrawals can be detrimental in the long run. The amount you take out of your account will count as income and incur a tax. On top of that, there is a 10 percent penalty if you are younger than 59½. And for six months after the withdrawal, the account is essentially frozen: Neither you nor your employer can contribute any money to your account.

A less damaging act would be to take a loan from your account. Most plans allow employees to do this for any reason. But there is a law forbidding employees from bor-rowing more than $50,000 or half of the vested account balance, whichever is less. Depending on the provider, the interest rate tends to be low. Loans must be repaid with after-tax money plus the interest, typically within five years. If you leave your job before the loan is repaid—or if you lose your job, as is more likely in this economy—you will have to pay off the balance soon after or incur an income tax and 10 percent penalty. Also, some plans will require that you reduce or eliminate new contributions to your 401(k) while you have an outstanding loan.

With either of these options, your money will be pulled out of the market, which over time reduces the size of your nest egg.

Unfortunately, more American workers are tapping into their retirement savings to pay off debt or save their homes from foreclosure. Vanguard, Fidelity, and T. Rowe Price all reported increases in hardship withdrawals at the beginning of 2009. That said, all three providers pointed out that the percentage of participants taking such a drastic step is low—below 2 percent.

"With the increase in credit card debt, with the increase in plan holders and the availability of borrowing against a 401(k), I think that society is starting to view it as more than a retirement plan, but as kind of like an alternative way to get cash," said Pamela Villarreal, senior policy analyst for the National Center for Policy Analysis in Dallas.

I have to say, given my financial situation, I have been tempted many times to withdraw money from my 401(k), but I kept hearing my planner's voice. "A last resort," she has repeatedly called it.

As bad as things have seemed lately, I don't want them to be worse later on in life.

Retirement Planning on Your Own

Some of you may work for companies that don't offer 401(k)-style plans. A good alternative for you would be an IRA. There are several varieties: Roth, traditional, SEP IRA, rollover, etc. The Roth and traditional are the ones you will hear about the most. Open these through a discount brokerage firm such as Vanguard, Fidelity, or Charles Schwab.

Roth IRA

This is a tax-exempt account, meaning you contribute your after-tax earnings but don't pay the IRS when you withdraw the money. You can pull out money you've contributed to it at any time without taxes or penalties. You do incur taxes and penalties if you withdraw investment income before you are 59½ or if the Roth is open less than five years; with a few exceptions. There are maximum contribution and income limits with the Roth.

In 2010, the contribution limit is $5,000 if you are forty-nine or younger ($6,000 if you are older).

If your modified adjusted gross income, a specific calculation on IRS tax form 1040, is above $105,000 for single filers or above $167,000 for married people filing jointly, the maximum amount you can contribute to your Roth starts to decrease. If your income is above $120,000 as a single person or $176,000 as married filing jointly, you won't qualify for a Roth at all.

If you qualify, this is a great option even if you can get a 401(k) through your employer. A good strategy would be to contribute as much as you need to your 401(k) to get your company's match, then put the rest of your retirement savings in a Roth IRA. Given the choice between a 401(k) in which your employer does not match your contribution and a Roth IRA, go with the Roth because you won't be taxed when you take out the money.

"You get no tax deduction now but when it grows to $50,000, it comes out completely tax-free," Ken Clark, a financial planner who writes for About.com, said. "For young people who are probably going to be in a higher tax bracket in retirement than they are out of college, they're going to come out way ahead using a Roth IRA compared to a traditional 401(k) that is not matched."

Traditional IRA

This is similar to the 401(k). It is a tax-deferred account. Depending on how much you make and whether or not your company has a retirement plan, you might be able to contribute before-tax earnings. But be prepared to contribute after-tax dollars.

When you take the money out at retirement, you will have to pay taxes on your before-tax contributions and the investment income. Additionally, you don't have the flexibility of withdrawing money at any time without incurring a penalty and income tax.

At 70½, you generally can no longer make contributions and must withdraw money annually. Neither rule applies to a Roth. A provision of the American Recovery and Reinvestment Act of 2009 temporarily eliminated this requirement in 2009.

For 2010, you can contribute a maximum of $5,000 to a traditional IRA if you are forty-nine or younger.

SEP IRA

This is often used by small business owners or self-employed individuals. This allows the employer to make retirement plan contributions to a traditional IRA in the employee's name rather than to a pension fund account in the company's name.

Self-Directed IRA

This is managed by the account holder rather than a third party. If you opt for this, you will have to make your own investment decisions.

Rollover IRA

When you leave a job, you have to decide what to do with your 401(k). Many young people take the cash and go. But there are better options. You can let your former employer hold onto it. You can open an account with your new employer. Or you can roll it over into this type of IRA, which means that you won't be limited to your new employer's 401(k) investment options.

My Retirement

My company has a very generous 401(k) program. The *Post* will match on a dollar-for-dollar basis the first 5 percent of my base salary that I put into my 401(k). In other words, if I set aside 5 percent of what I make before taxes, the *Post* will give me another 5 percent. Talk about free money.

It's too bad the market was free-falling and I was losing that money.

Christine, my planner, kept pushing me to review my 401(k). It was the end of 2008, and I have to admit I resisted. My friends and coworkers were avoiding their 401(k) statements. Even some of my editors were.

I wanted to remain happily oblivious. But Christine would never let me be oblivious about my finances.

I followed her orders. As of February 28, 2009, my account was down almost 15 percent year-to-date.

To determine my risk tolerance, Christine instructed me to take the investors' questionnaire on my 401(k) provider's website.

I logged onto Vanguard.com and proceeded to answer the eleven questions. Among them:

Question: From September 2008 through November 2008, stocks lost over 31 percent. If I owned a stock investment that lost about 31 percent in three months, I would:

1. Sell all of the remaining assets.
2. Sell some of the remaining assets.
3. Hold on to the investment and sell nothing.
4. Buy more of the investment.

Being a personal finance writer, I knew what financial planners *want* their clients to answer. The good test-taker in me was tempted to click on that third answer, even though I had not exactly been feeling that way during those months. In school, if I ever scored anything below a ninety—actually more like a ninety-five—on an exam, I would shed tears. I'm not exaggerating. I was one of those annoyingly competitive students.

But I answered: Sell some of the remaining assets.

At the end of the questionnaire, Vanguard said that my target asset mix would be nothing in short-term reserves, 30 percent in bonds, and 70 percent in stocks.

If I used the method of subtracting my age from one hundred, I should invest 68 percent of my portfolio in stocks. The two were pretty much in synch.

I was not. I had 9.6 percent in short-term reserves, 29.4 percent in bonds, and only 61 percent in stocks.

"An aggressive investor would be 80 percent in stocks and 20 percent in bonds," Christine said. "A conservative one would be 20 percent in stocks and 80 percent in fixed-income. Moderate would be 60 percent stocks and 40 percent bonds."

Be more aggressive, Vanguard was telling me.

Over coffee at Starbucks one morning, Christine and I reviewed my contributions. She had run an analysis of my portfolio.

My short-term reserves were stored in a money market fund. Almost 10 percent of my portfolio balance was tied up in that. A money market would preserve my principal but not give me much of a return.

Of the 61 percent I had in stocks, 29.1 percent of that was invested in my company. "Keep in mind that a heavy weighting in one company's stock could increase your investment risk," the Vanguard website had pointed out to me.

Christine found other trouble spots in my portfolio.

I did not have enough in international stocks, she said.

"Aren't they doing poorly?" I asked. Most international stocks were tanking even faster than domestic ones at that point.

"They're doing worse, but you're buying in when it's low," she said.

Many financial planners argue that there are good buying opportunities even when the market is down. There are plenty of sound companies selling for much less than they used to that seem sure to rebound in a few years.

I wasn't the type to bottom-fish, which is the term used for the act of gobbling up cheap stocks just because they're cheap. I had learned, from many interviews with financial planners, that you shouldn't buy a stock just because the price is right. You should first do an in-depth analysis of the company to determine if it has solid leaders and business practices that can sustain it through economic upheaval.

Christine wasn't suggesting that I bottom-fish, but she did think my portfolio could be better diversified.

"I believe in strategic asset allocation," she said.

My strategy, apparently, was totally off. I didn't really have a strategy. Frankly, I think I had let an ex-boyfriend pick my investments years ago because I thought he knew more about finance than I did. We broke up soon after.

I had too much invested in information technology, Christine said. I had too little in "value," as opposed to "growth." Value companies sell at bargain prices and pay dividends (regular payments) to investors while growth companies are fast-growing and may pay no or little to no dividends, instead putting their profits back into the company. I had a lot in mid-cap, or medium-sized, companies and too little in large-cap, or larger, companies. A properly diversified portfolio would have more in large-cap, a little less in mid-cap, and even less in small-cap, Christine told me.

Oddly enough, my investments were outperforming the S&P 500. In other words, I was doing better than a good chunk of the market. But that was kind of a fluke, Christine said.

"Sometimes we find our returns are better than the S&P 500 but we're taking too much risk," she said.

Wait a second, I said. "I'm taking too much risk right now?" I asked. I thought the problem was that I was too conservative. I mean, I have a lot of my money in low-risk short-term bonds.

She nodded. My lack of diversification was putting my savings in danger. Investors face numerous types of investment risks, such as market and industry fluctuations. Selecting different types of assets and diversifying may help reduce the risk of your overall investment portfolio.

"You don't want to be concentrated in one sector such as information technology or financial services, or concentrated in only short-term bonds. You don't want to own more mid-cap than large-cap securities. Yes, there might be international risk but you might benefit from a little more exposure long-term. You have some fixed income and cash equivalents. I have to believe that's what sheltered you," she said.

Then she told me how expensive my funds were—as in, how much I was paying the managers to manage them.

Funds are more expensive if they're actively managed. That's why mutual funds tend to be pricey. The managers are frequently buying and selling stocks and bonds as they try to outperform a benchmark. Index funds are less expensive because they follow a benchmark and do not require the same level of professional management and research. My Sequoia stock fund, for instance, had a 1 percent operating expense ratio, meaning that each year Sequoia would charge me $1 for every $100 I invested with them. My Vanguard 500 Index Fund Investor Shares stock fund had a low .15 percent operating expense ratio, meaning Vanguard would charge me only 15 cents for every $100.

At this point, I was feeling overwhelmed. Too much information, I thought. I was too polite to say that. After all, she was giving me the most thorough analysis I had ever received on my investments.

I resolved to take her advice. Diversify, diversify, diversify.

Christine could tell I had had enough for one morning. "For you, you have time," she said in her soothing voice.

Time I definitely have. Given the sorry state of my retirement savings, I was looking at a good thirty-five to forty years of work ahead of me.

It's a good thing I like my job. All I had to hope for was that the newspaper industry would last that long.

fourteen
what do you expect when you didn't expect it?

Sylvia Raymond is twenty-seven and has gone without health insurance for eight years. She has two part-time jobs in her Ohio town, neither of which offers coverage. She doesn't get annual physical exams and has been to the dentist only a handful of times. Because Stephanie has no insurance, her ten-year-old daughter also has gone uncovered for much of her life. When her daughter broke her arm, Sylvia paid $1,000 for visits to the emergency room and to an orthopedic specialist.

"When it comes to emergencies like that, you don't have a choice," she told me when I called her in early 2009.

Soon after, she got online and found individual health insurance for about $90 a month. But she was a single mom earning little as a part-time nail technician at a salon and a part-time admissions clerk at a hospital. She let the insurance lapse. "The expense of it has always held me back," she said.

To be young and uninsured is common. In an analysis of census data, the Commonwealth Fund, a health-advocacy group, found that people between the ages of nineteen and twenty-nine were one of the largest segments of the U.S. population without health insurance. In 2007,

13.2 million lacked coverage. More than half of eighteen-to thirty-four-year-olds surveyed by Qvisory, an advocacy organization that helps young adults with financial issues, had gone uninsured at some point in the past five years, and 28 percent had unpaid medical bills.

Insurance companies typically drop children from their parents' plans when they turn eighteen or nineteen or graduate from college. When they leave college, many graduates work temporary, freelance, or part-time jobs that offer no insurance. If they're lucky, their colleges will offer interim insurance. Some states force insurers to cover grown children on their parents' policies until their mid-twenties or even thirty if they have no coverage through their jobs or have no jobs. They have to be unmarried and live in the same state, but not the same house, as their parents.

For those who are employed, having access to health insurance doesn't necessarily mean they will take it. Nearly one-fifth of young singles surveyed by the National Associ-ation of Insurance Commissioners said they would decline employer health insurance to save money. Cash-strapped and earning little, they reason that they are young and healthy enough to go without. They fail—or refuse—to recognize that accidents happen. With the cost of medical care soaring, these "young invincibles," as the health indus-try has dubbed them, are taking a huge risk.

"If they have any kind of medical catastrophe, it will be financial hardship the rest of their lives. You really in our world cannot afford to be irresponsible about this," said Etti Baranoff, associate professor of insurance and finance at Virginia Commonwealth University. "And you know how many young people pay $5 a month to insure their stupid cell phones?"

The health insurance world is a Byzantine one. Even those of us who are insured do not fully comprehend it. Each year, around October, I receive a packet in the mail with the word *OPEN* written in huge letters on the envelope. For many years, I simply checked off the same boxes I had the previous year. But in 2008, I found myself paying a lot more out of pocket for doctors' visits and prescriptions. A stress fracture in my left foot, caused by regular running, forced me to see a podiatrist several times. I let him make me a pair of special pads to support the arch in my foot. Soon after, I was slapped with a nearly $400 bill. Then a mystery pain in my stomach one weekend sent me to the ER. I can't even tell you how much that cost because the charges did not arrive in one easy-to-follow bill. For the next few months, I received countless statements detailing what I owed after my company covered its share. The charges ranged from $10 for a pill to hundreds of dollars for an abdominal CT scan.

Even I, with my fancy college degree, cannot decipher all the statements I get from my doctors and from Aetna, which administers my health plan. The best thing I, and all you young adults out there, can do is teach ourselves as much as we can about the health insurance world, especially now that our employers, many of them ailing in this economy, are asking us to assume more of the cost.

"In reality, in this country, most people know more about their car insurance than they do about their health insurance," said Sam Gibbs, senior vice president of eHealth-Insurance, a website that compares health care plans for consumers. "If you spend a half hour and get the basics then you have the opportunity to make an intelligent decision."

I took Gibbs' advice and started with the basics.

Your Health Care Glossary

A few terms keep coming up when you talk about health insurance. I wanted to understand what they all meant.

Premium: The cost of your insurance plan. If you get your insurance through your employer, you will split the premium with the company. A premium can be paid monthly, quarterly, or annually.

Deductible: The dollar amount you pay out of pocket for covered services before your health insurance kicks in.

Co-Payment: Commonly referred to as a *co-pay*, this is a flat dollar amount you must contribute for medical services such as office visits, lab work, or prescription drugs. Co-insurance is your percentage share of the cost of these services. You might have to pay this in addition to a deductible. There is almost always an "out-of-pocket limit," or a cap on the consumer's cost-sharing responsibility.

The ABCs — or HMOs, PPOs, and POSs — of Health Care

I have many quirks. One of them is that I am a bit of a hypochondriac. When I feel any sort of pain, I rush to my computer, Google my symptoms, and pronounce to all my friends that I've got a horrible disease. I don't calm down until I see my doctor and make her prove that I don't have that disease. I don't miss any annual exams. After having braces in high school, I don't skimp on my dental care either. I'm not one of those people who believe lots of water and rest will take care of any ailment. If there is a drug made to get rid of it, I will take it.

That's why I went with the Aetna Preferred Provider Organization (PPO) when I got to the *Post*, even though it was the more expensive plan. My other options were Health Maintenance Organizations (HMOs). I didn't know much about HMOs but I knew that they were too restrictive.

After a lot of research, I learned that there are three main types of health insurance: traditional, managed care, and consumer-directed. Dental, vision, mental health, and prescription drug coverage are also usually included.

1. *Traditional Plans:* You can choose any health care provider you want and pay a fee for each service you receive from that doctor or hospital. Either you or the provider then submits a claim to your insurer for a reimbursement. If the provider charges more than the insurance company is willing to pay, you make up the difference.

2. *Managed Care Plans:* More than half of Americans have a managed care plan that revolves around a network of physicians and hospitals with which the insurance company has negotiated rates. If you stick with a provider in the network, you pay less out of your own pocket. If you go with one outside the network, you pay more. Typically, the more

expensive the plan is, the more flexibility you have in choosing your doctors. There are three major types of managed care plans:

- *Health Maintenance Organization (HMO):* You select a primary care physician (PCP) from a list of network providers. The PCP manages your care and refers you to specialists if needed. The HMO will typically not cover any treatment received from an out-of-network physician. But if you only see your doctor for your annual exam and don't get sick often, this might not be a bad option.
- *Preferred Provider Organization (PPO):* With this plan, you don't have a primary care physician who manages all your care and decides whether or not you can see a specialist. However, even though you can go straight to a specialist if you want to, that specialist has to be within your network, otherwise you will pay a higher deductible or co-payment.
- *Point-of-Service (POS):* This is essentially a hybrid of a PPO and an HMO. Like an HMO, you have to choose a primary care physician. Like a PPO, you can go to an out-of-network doctor and incur more of the cost. That is, unless the primary care physician refers you to that out-of-network doctor, in which case you don't get hit with huge out-of-pocket expenses. And you pay a higher premium.

3. *Consumer-Directed or Consumer-Choice Health Plans:* These were designed to give you more

flexibility. They usually combine a high-deductible health plan with a Health Savings Account (HSA) or a Health Reimbursement Arrangement (HRA). They include an account you manage yourself. Your choices are:

- *Health Savings Account (HSA):* You must be covered by a high-deductible health plan to qualify for this. You and/or your employer can contribute to this account up to a certain amount. The contributions are tax-deductible and earn tax-free interest. In some cases, you can also contribute tax-free dollars from your paycheck. You can either cover a qualified medical expense with it or withdraw cash. If you don't use it by the end of the year, it rolls over to the next. And if you leave your employer, you take it with you. But if you withdraw cash and don't spend it on a qualified medical expense, it becomes taxable and subject to other penalties.
- *Health Reimbursement Arrangement:* Your employer funds this account. Generally, you use it to pay deductibles and co-insurance under the health care plan provided by your company. In some cases, you can use it for other qualified medical expenses. Unused funds can be carried over from year to year. But if you leave the plan, you leave your money behind.
- *Flexible Spending Account (FSA):* This third option can be used with either a consumer-directed health plan or a traditional plan. Money is taken from your

paycheck, pretax, and deposited into this account. You can use that money for any qualified medical expense, as determined by the IRS. The list of qualified medical expenses is actually quite large. Even a container of Advil counts. It's tax-free money. But be careful how much you contribute because you lose it if you don't use it by the end of the year. Also, if you leave your employer, you lose your FSA money.

Time for a Checkup

A couple of years ago, my employer replaced the Aetna PPO with an Aetna HealthFund. I didn't want to be bothered with the research, assumed it was similar to what I had before, and accepted it. As it turned out, it wasn't all that similar.

With my finances in shambles and Open Enrollment season in full swing, I finally downloaded the 117-page document my company made available to us to understand our health insurance options. I had three options: the Aetna HealthFund or two HMOs.

This is how my HealthFund works. My employer pays for the first $1,000 of my medical and prescription costs each year (the dollar amount is higher for those with families). Once the "fund" is exhausted, I have to pay all expenses until I meet my total deductible, which because I am single is $2,000 (part of my deductible could have been covered by the fund as well). Once that deductible is met, my company and I proceed to share the costs, the plan paying 90 percent for a provider within the network and 70 percent out of network. There is also an annual co-insurance limit. All my preventative visits are 100 percent covered.

In November 2008, I had to make a choice: Continue with my plan or go with an HMO?

Choosing a Plan

There are a number of factors you should consider when deciding on a plan, said Tracey Baker, coauthor of *Navigating Your Health Benefits for Dummies*. Is it affordable? Are you getting the type of coverage you need? If you have children, does it provide good coverage for them? If you're dealing with a network of health care providers, how extensive is it? Are any of those providers near your home or work? Does your plan have a good website, or will you constantly have to call the customer service line to get answers to your questions?

Go back and assess your health needs during the previous year, Baker said. How many times did you see your doctor? How many prescriptions did you have filled? Were they ongoing or one-time-use prescriptions? Do you have any recurring illnesses? Do you have any hobbies like running marathons that could put you at risk for injuries?

Then think about possible life changes in the upcoming year. Do you intend to get married? If you are married, are you planning to have children? Do you think you'll finally get that knee surgery you've been putting off for a while?

"It comes down to cost and benefit. Every benefit and every bit of flexibility has a cost. It comes down to knowing what your options are and looking ahead and looking back," said Baker, who is also a certified financial planner and vice president of CJM Wealth Advisors in Fairfax, Virginia.

Matthew J. McDermott, an employee benefits consultant at Landmark Group of Brighton, in Rochester, New York, said if you do have a chronic condition or take prescription drugs regularly, you should look at plans with lower deductibles that include prescription coverage and specialist visits at a lower co-pay. If you don't have such needs, look at plans with a higher deductible that protect against unexpected illnesses or injuries. This is sometimes known as catastrophic coverage. A higher deductible means you pay a lower premium.

Keep in mind that you are not obligated to take your employer's insurance if you find a good deal on your own. If you're married and your spouse has a better plan, perhaps you can piggyback off that. Maybe you can find a good individual health plan online or through an insurance broker. The good thing about this is that if you get laid off, you take your insurance with you.

If you go with your employer's plan and don't like it, Open Enrollment will come again soon enough.

What If Your Employer Does Not Offer Coverage or You Are Self-Employed?

Things get even more complicated when you must shop for your own plan. Don't fret: Your youth and good health will work in your favor. Insurance companies want you because you don't cost them as much.

There are many websites, such as eHealthInsurance .com, that compare various insurers. They can also help you find dental and vision coverage. To save time, consider using an insurance broker, paid by the health plan, but make sure he or she works with several different companies.

If you had been with an employer who offered insurance, and you were pleased with it, try that insurer first.

If that's not an option, check with your state's or county's health department. All states, by federal law, have to offer some health insurance to people who are uninsurable. It's not inexpensive but it's there.

If you are low-income, you might qualify for free patient programs, services at clinics, or other types of government programs. If you are unemployed and fall below a certain income threshold, you could qualify for Medicaid.

Think about purchasing coverage through a professional, alumni, or trade organization or a local Chamber of Commerce. Even civic and church groups have group plans.

Whatever you decide, make sure you get at least enough coverage to cover any major, catastrophic event. "That could be devastating when you don't have a lot of money and you don't have much saved," Baker said.

Sylvia, the uninsured twenty-seven-year-old, knows that a medical catastrophe could leave her bankrupt. Luckily, she has been healthy so far, despite the lack of preventative care. "Of course, anything can happen—I'm not invincible. I could have a big emergency. There have been medical bills that have gone unpaid. I'll send something when I can and then I forget about it. It's always a worry."

When I talked to her last, she had recently gotten married and was hoping to get on her husband's plan. She's got to do something: When I spoke to her in early 2009, she had recently learned that she was pregnant.

What If You Have Been Laid Off or Are Between Jobs?

COBRA is perhaps the best-sounding acronym I have come across so far. This stands for Consolidated Omnibus Budget Reconciliation Act, the landmark legislation passed in 1986 that allows laid-off employees to continue their former employer's health care coverage for up to eighteen months. As it was written, the law requires the employees to pay the full premium plus a 2 percent administrative fee, which makes it unaffordable to people who have just lost their jobs.

Shana Astrachan, thirty-four, can attest to that. In 2007, she was laid off from a small design and manufacturing company in San Francisco. Because she has asthma, she could not afford to go without insurance. So she opted for COBRA, which raised her monthly premium to about $270 a month, substantially higher than what she was paying before. She had no regular income and was trying to start her own jewelry design business.

"It was a lot. I live by myself in a one-bedroom apartment that is relatively expensive even though I've been here six years, and it's rent-controlled. You've got to sell a lot of work to pay rent and all the other expenses of starting a business," she said.

When her COBRA ran out after eighteen months, she logged onto eHealthInsurance.com to search for a replacement. She checked out several companies, but in the end settled for the same one that insured her through her previous employer. The coverage is more limited and doctor's visits cost her more, but she was able to keep all her doctors and pays less per month.

"I was happy to get off of COBRA and have the security of having my own health insurance plan," she said.

There is good news for people like Shana. In February 2009, President Obama signed into law an economic stimulus package that subsidizes 65 percent of COBRA premiums for employees laid off through 2009.

Another option for the laid-off is to purchase temporary coverage. Major insurers sell temporary plans for one to twelve months. They aren't necessarily better than COBRA and tend to have high deductibles, but they are less expensive.

What's in a Name?

The pharmaceutical industry has led us to believe that brand-name drugs are always better than generics. Not true!

The Food and Drug Administration stipulates that a generic drug must be the same as its brand-name version in "dosage, safety, strength, how it is taken, quality, performance and intended use."

When your doctor hands you a prescription, ask if you can go with the generic, which is usually much cheaper. If your doctor prescribes you a drug that does not have a generic version, ask your pharmacist if there is a similar, cheaper alternative, then confirm it with your doctor.

Consider filling your prescriptions though the mail.

Many programs will give you a two or three months' supply for the price of one. If you have insurance, see if your health plan has a deal with pharmacy benefit managers such as Express Scripts, Caremark, or Medco, which process drug claims and often give discounts if you order medication through the mail. Even if you don't have insurance, these companies have good mail-order programs.

There are also legitimate online pharmacies that can save you money. The National Association of Boards of Pharmacies (www.nabp.net) recommends that patients only use sites accredited through its Verified Internet Pharmacy Practice Sites (VIPPS) program. Many illegitimate online pharmacies, often operating overseas, peddle expired or fake drugs.

Finally, go to your local Wal-Mart, Neighborhood Market, or Sam's Club pharmacy. They have a $4 Prescriptions Program. That's $4 for a thirty-day supply and $10 for a ninety-day supply. Kmart has a similar program.

Tuning Up Your Mind

We've all had moments in our lives when we've considered seeing, or gone to see, a therapist. I've had quite a few.

Many health plans cover mental health visits, but you often have to pay a higher deductible, co-pay, or co-insurance.

Another option is your company's Employee Assistance Program (EAP) if it has one. Usually, you call the EAP hotline and a representative finds you a participating therapist or counselor. Your employer will cover the cost for a certain number of visits. It's confidential so you don't have to worry that your boss is going to find out.

I used the *Post*'s EAP after my last breakup. I was referred to a therapist near my apartment who often worked with couples. As I told him the story of finding my live-in boyfriend in a hotel room with another woman while I thought he was in Iraq, he couldn't stop shaking his head.

"That's the worst breakup story I've ever heard," he said.

I felt better after a few sessions.

Long-Term Disability Insurance or Life Insurance?

When you're in your twenties and thirties, you have a better chance of becoming disabled than dying.

If your employer offers long-term disability insurance, take it. If you have the option of buying life insurance, I can't tell you exactly what to do because it depends on your situation. But most experts agree that at this point in your life, if you had to choose between the two, go with the long-term disability insurance.

"Statistics show that someone is more likely to be disabled before sixty-five, but more people buy life insurance than long-term disability insurance," said Dov Eisenberger, president of Vital Edge Insurance Agency, in New York. "They're insuring their gold, their watches, their houses, but they don't want to insure their income and that's a mistake."

If you're out of work for several months, and you have long-term disability insurance, you will receive a certain percentage of your monthly salary to cover your living costs. If your employer does not offer this, you can buy a policy in the open market. For the women reading this, pay attention! Some employers don't grant paid maternity leave. Fear not: You can use your long-term disability instead.

Life insurance is a lot more complicated. Many employers give you basic life insurance at no cost. My company covers me for a full year's salary. That's perfectly adequate, as my planner pointed out. I don't have children. I have debt, but not more than one year's salary's worth. If I die, my debts would be paid off. Sure, my family would be sad, but no children or other dependents would be left behind struggling without my income.

Too often, young single people get roped into buying expensive life insurance policies that cover you for your entire life. If you're young and have children, you have to make sure your family is taken care of if you die. That doesn't mean you have to be covered forever. You can try what is known as a term life insurance policy for twenty or thirty years. That should be enough to get your kids through college if they lose you.

My Turn to Make a Call

Gathering all this information has actually been a big help to me. Before I did all this research, I knew very little about my health insurance.

With Open Enrollment nearing its end in late 2008, I had to make a decision between the HealthFund and an HMO. It was a tough call. I had been seeing the same general practitioner, dermatologist, and gynecologist for years. Given how often I see doctors, did I really want to search for a whole new slate of health care professionals? The last time I saw Dr. Agrawal, my general practitioner, she walked in with her laptop chronicling all my visits over all these years, took one look at me, and said "Oh no. You're not well. You never look this bad." True enough, I had bronchitis. I adore Dr. Agrawal. She gets me.

With an HMO, however, I wouldn't have to deal with deductibles or co-insurance. I would only have co-pays.

I think back now to what Shana Astrachan had to say. She considered several insurance companies. They all had something good to offer. But in the end, she stuck with the insurer she had at her previous job. "The time I would spend finding someone else, finding new prescriptions and doctors? The money is worth not having to think about it," she said.

I too was not yet ready to dump my doctors. That could change the next time I get that Open Enrollment packet. But for now, I feel good knowing that when I walk into my doctor's office, she'll be able to tell right away when something is wrong.

fifteen
papa don't preach...unless he's paying my rent

For a while, everything was going right for Rick Schram. He had been working at Macy's for two years when he was promoted to director of loss prevention at stores in east central Florida near Melbourne. He was pleased with his salary, about $40,000 a year. He was also newly engaged. "Life was grand," he said.

And so Rick and his fiancée decided to upgrade. They concluded their apartment was too small and rented a 2,200-square-foot house. It seemed like a good idea. The apartment cost them $925 a month while the house would cost $890. What they failed to calculate was the added expense of 1,000 square feet more. They bought new furniture. There was no washer or dryer so they got new machines, driving up the electricity and water bills. It was manageable at first, and they were happy, so they splurged a bit too much, going on fishing trips and eating at expensive restaurants.

It was only manageable because Rick was partially financing their lifestyle with his credit card. But it wasn't his only debt. He also had $25,000 in student loans and a $440 monthly car payment. His fiancée's smaller salary helped but not enough. One month they couldn't cover their electricity and cable bills. Then they couldn't make rent. "It just snowballed," he said.

Their relationship started to crumble under the strain. Then in October 2008, the owner of the house they were renting was foreclosed on, and Rick and his fiancée were ordered out. They didn't have enough money to move or secure a new rental.

Rick's father Richard remembers the phone call. He had already lent his son some money. "We need to do something. Your mother and I are not going to put more money into this," Richard recalls telling his son.

Rick admits to relying too heavily on his parents. "When I was running into problems, I thought 'My dad makes a comfortable living. He could help me out.'"

I could sense Rick's embarrassment in admitting this. I told him that not long ago I had to have a similar conversation with my parents.

Rick's engagement ended and by November, he was living in his parents' 520-square-foot garage apartment in Winter Park, about ninety minutes from Melbourne. The move back home meant he had a three-hour commute each way every day, but at least he wasn't paying rent.

Rick never thought he would end up back home at age thirty-one. His father and mother, aged sixty-eight and sixty-four, were done raising their three children and thought they could enjoy their time alone.

"There's a feeling in him of 'I wish I didn't have to be here but what else am I going to do?' The feeling on behalf of the parents is 'Gee, I wish you weren't here, but we are your parents and we want to help you'" said Richard, who, ironically, works for the Consumer Credit Counseling Service in Orlando.

Gone are the days when college graduation meant getting your own apartment and breaking free from Mom and Dad. The bad economy, loss of jobs, high cost of living, and growing student loan and credit card debt are forcing many adult children to rely more heavily on their parents. Some are moving back in. Others are simply borrowing money.

"You've got a couple of forces working together to revive intergenerational ties in a way that is different from the past," said Stephanie Coontz, director of public education and research for the Council on Contemporary Families, a Chicago-based nonprofit.

These boomerang kids, as sociologists and psychologists call them, are the latest change in the ever-shifting landscape of the American family. Intergenerational families—parents, their children, and sometimes grandparents all in one household—were not uncommon in the nineteenth century. That changed in the early part of the twentieth century, when sons and daughters married younger—sometimes in their teens—and quickly moved out to create their own households. By the 1960s, as more men and women opted for college and careers, the average age of marriage started creeping up. Without spouses, many adults found it difficult to cut the so-called silver cord that tied them to their parents. For a while, a thriving economy allowed them to remain emotionally tied but somewhat financially independent.

"In the past twenty or thirty years, the rising age of marriage has led more kids to spend a longer time in college and exploring with jobs outside of marriage," Koontz said. "Many of these kids feel free to move in with their parents and even if they don't, they feel closer to them because parents are a support for them emotionally and financially."

According to the 2007 U.S. census, 55 percent of men and 48 percent of women between the ages of eighteen and twenty-four lived with their parents.

Researchers for the Network on Transitions to Adulthood, a group financed by the John D. and Catherine T. MacArthur Foundation, found that since the 1970s, the number of twentysomethings living with their parents has increased by 50 percent. Of those who moved out of the house by age twenty-two, 16 percent returned home before they hit thirty-five, the researchers found.

Recession will likely only accelerate the growth of the phenomenon, as many college graduates find themselves in a market where jobs are not available or don't pay as well as they expected when they took out expensive loans. Almost half of June 2008's college graduates planned to move back home after their graduation, according to a survey by the employment website Monster.com.

It's not just housing that adult children are accepting from their parents, but cash or cosigned loans. In a Pew Research Center 2006 survey, 68 percent of baby boomer parents said they were providing financial support to at least one adult child.

Some research suggests that baby boomers want to coddle their children well into adulthood, which is why today's parents are so willing to support their grown-up kids. They know what the generations before them—those who grew up during the Great Depression and World War II—had to withstand, and have drawn lessons from that, but they don't want their children to go through similar hardship.

"I really think it comes back to the parents forgetting something the grandparents' generation knew, which is that adversity is not necessarily a bad thing. Struggle with adversity is how character develops," said Aaron Cooper, a clinical psychologist at the Family Institute at Northwestern University and author of *I Just Want My Kids to Be Happy: Why You Shouldn't Say It, Why You Shouldn't Think It, What You Should Embrace Instead*. "That so-called Greatest Generation wasn't labeled the Greatest Generation because they sat on a comfortable cushion their whole lives."

I didn't really grow up with a pair of baby boomer parents. My father is eighty and my mother is somewhere in her mid- to late sixties. They didn't coddle me in the sense that they would constantly ask me about what was going on in school or in my love life. I don't blame them. When could they? We were hardly ever all in the same house together. We hardly ate meals together as a family. They never went to my school functions because they worked so many hours. They never helped me with my homework because they couldn't read English as well as I could. It didn't matter much. Each semester or quarter I would show up with straight As or high nineties. They smiled, congratulated me, and signed the report card as required. As long as I delivered the grades, they were happy to let me be.

But there is an intimacy among members of many immigrant families that is quite unique. The intergenerational family is a given in many of these households, especially among Latinos. That's how it was back in their homelands. My brother, who is six years older than I am, is unmarried and has yet to move out. My sister is married and lives not too far away from my parents in Queens. My brother-in-law's mother, sister, and niece live together in a house around the corner from them. My mother takes care of my sister's children. They all get together every weekend for meals.

I am the only one who left Queens. I've been gone for about fifteen years now, and until I get married, my parents still expect me to return to New York someday, get a job at the *New York Times* or *Daily News* and sleep in the bedroom that has remained unchanged since my childhood.

"My poor little girl. You're all abandoned there in DC. There's no one to take care of you," my father says, as he rubs my hair, every time I visit him.

When I called them in need of money, there was no doubt what their answer would be. Part of me believes they enjoyed helping me. I had proved their point, that I was indeed, all abandoned. I'm not saying that they relished my trouble. But I think they miss the kind of relationship they have with my other two siblings, whom they talk to or see almost every day. My parents don't travel. They don't go out much. Their lives revolve around their children and their grandchildren. For a while now, they have felt that I was the child who didn't need them, and I think that made them sad. Here I was finally admitting that yes, I do need you. I really do need you.

But has our inability to cut the cord from our parents— be they baby boomers or immigrants—placed us all at risk?

"We have a big problem in this country where older generations bail out younger generations to a point where we handicap people from succeeding," said Ken Clark, a certified financial planner who also has a master's in counseling psychology.

Not only does it handicap us young people from succeeding but it also jeopardizes our parents' financial welfare, Clark argues. The more money they give us, the less they will have for their retirement, and many of them have already seen their savings dwindle with the dramatic declines in the stock market.

"Those children will be resilient. They have forty years ahead of them. Parents don't," said David Petersen, a certified financial planner and president of Financial Services Advisory, in Rockville, Maryland. "Think of an airplane. You, the parent, put the oxygen mask on you first then you help your infant children. You can't help your infant children if you can't breathe yourself. I think the same principle applies with adult kids."

Rick's parents have not asked for rent. In exchange for their hospitality, he helps maintain the house. Thankfully, he gets along with his parents and even calls his father his best friend.

Financial planners and psychologists say that as much as they love their children, parents have to set boundaries.

If they lend their children money, parents should specify if it is a loan or a gift. A loan should come with a contract that spells out terms of repayment. If their children move in, there should be a timetable for moving out. They also should decide if they're going to charge rent or ask that they contribute to household expenses.

Rick Schram and I commiserated over our arrangements with our parents.

"I feel bad. They're at an age where they had their children, and they want their own time," he said. His plan is to have his own place within a year. That's when he'll be done paying off his car. He also intends to see a credit counselor at his father's agency.

"It's the downfall of the Generation Xers," he said with a chuckle. I laughed too. "A lot of people in our generation, they lean on their parents too much. I have wonderful, wonderful parents. I knew if any of us had any problems we'd be welcomed back with open arms. That could be part of the problem...I had always had things given to me. I never actually appreciated it by going out and earning it on my own. It's partly my fault. I had too much of a comfort landing."

He stopped and thought for a while. "But they raised me to be a good person. I think I am a good person."

His father does not doubt that. "I feel bad for my son right now that he's found himself in this spot," Richard said.

When all three of his children left the house, Richard found himself thinking mostly about how he and his wife would manage their retirement when the time came. Now, he factors his son into their future. "If I retired and he lost his job, how would he survive? That may be kind of con-voluted thinking."

Both Rick and Richard admit that the arrangement has been awkward at times. For one thing, Richard and his wife normally go to bed around 10:00 p.m. But now that his son is living at home, Richard has trouble sleeping until he knows that he is home safely. One night, Rick didn't get home until 3:00 a.m. "When they're not living at home, you're not so concerned, but when they're living under your roof you get concerned," Richard said.

The family has also tiptoed around financial discussions. Richard has asked his son about his debt, but he can tell that Rick doesn't want to get into too many details.

"Because he is an adult it's kind of hard to say, well, who do you owe that kind of money to? You find out when he wants you to find out," Richard said.

Rick knows he is indebted to his parents and tries not to blow them off when they ask questions. "I have to respect them," he said.

I too have tried to be honest with my parents about my finances, as embarrassing as it has been.

Shortly after I borrowed money from my parents, I had planned to go to New York for a weekend but got stuck in DC because I had to work. I called my mother to let her know I would not make it. She was obviously disappointed. After a few more minutes of conversation, she said, "The next time you come to New York, we need to sit down and have a serious conversation about your finances."

"Are you mad at me?" I asked, suddenly sounding like a sixteen-year-old.

"No, you're my daughter. I could never be mad at you," she assured me. "We all make mistakes. You just have to learn from them."

It hurt my parents to see their youngest child in trouble. And it hurt me to know that I had failed them.

Of their three children, I was the one who was supposed to excel. I was the only one with a college degree and a career.

My sister Lucy didn't want to go to college. She wanted to be married and raise a family. And she has excelled at that. In 1998, soon after I graduated from college, she married another Ecuadorean who grew up in Queens. She was twenty-seven. Her husband is generous, sweet, smart, and hardworking. He treats her, my two nephews, and my parents with all the love and respect they deserve. She did clerical work for a few years at a hospital in Manhattan. But when she and her husband were financially stable, she quit to focus on her sons.

Unlike me, she did not spend thousands of dollars on a college degree, yet she is the more financially stable of the two of us. She even made the wiser real estate move. My mother helped her and her husband buy a house when they got married. That house is now worth hundreds of thousands of dollars more than it was when they bought it.

You can argue that she is the more stable of the two of us, period. She has been married to the same man for more than a decade. I, on the other hand, have lived with two different men in nine years.

Not only had I not achieved my American Dream of

exploring the world while succeeding at my career, spending quality time with my family and friends, having wonderful love affairs, and not going broke, but I had also not allowed my parents to achieve their American Dream of working hard to make sure their children were financially and emotionally secure. I later did take a loan from my parents to cover a credit card that had a substantial interest rate hike—credit card issuers have increasingly been raising rates and fees during the economic downturn—but I made sure the terms of the repayment were clear and that I would reimburse them when other funds became available. I struggled with the decision until my parents and a friend who had done the same thing reasoned it was the best option for the time being.

In the throes of my shame at having to turn to my parents for help, I turned to my editor for advice. I was near tears as I told him about my financial troubles over coffee. I told him how guilty I felt about taking their money. He later sent me a comforting message. "Your parents really are doing it because they love you and want to help and it makes them feel good," he wrote.

And that's what my parents have told me over and over again. But someday, when they are older and unable to take care of themselves, I would like to be stable enough to help them.

sixteen
show me the money

I've tried to cut back on things I don't need.

I used to have a full menu of cable TV. I cancelled it entirely for several months. Then I realized I really do need CNN so I resumed cable without the premium channels. In the old days, I would collect hats, shawls, purses, and other accessories. Now, whenever I get the urge to add to that collection, I remind myself of how many I already own. For a while, in a burst of nostalgia, I kept buying DVDs of my favorite TV shows growing up: *Dynasty*, *Little House on the Prairie*, *The Golden Girls*. I now only rent DVDs.

However, there are certain things I cannot give up: A skim vanilla latte from Starbucks a couple of times a week. A skim chai from Tryst, a coffeehouse in my neighborhood, once or twice a week. A few glasses of Sancerre and a couple of appetizers with my closest friends at my neighborhood bar. An occasional trip to the Middle East or Latin America. A trip to New York every couple of months to visit my family.

Unfortunately, all these things cost money. Cutting back on unnecessary expenses won't fill my bank account and pay off my debt. And I probably won't be getting a raise for a while because of the state of my industry. I could give up journalism for a higher-paying job, but I love it. There has to be another approach.

And there is: I got a book deal. After taxes and the small cut that my agent takes, however, my advance for this book won't take care of everything I owe on my credit cards and other creditors. It does make a dent, but I won't be debt-free.

In this economy, we all have to figure out ways to make more money. Our employers aren't going to give us raises and bonuses the way they used to. In fact, some of my friends are getting pay cuts. The cost of living isn't going to drop dramatically. I hate to say it, but some of us are going to get laid off and we need to make as much money as we can now to cushion that blow later.

For much of this book, I've talked about trimming expenses. But that's only part of what you can do to make yourself financially secure—and have some money left over to enjoy a few luxuries. Use your skills and talents to generate more money. For me, that skill was writing. For my brother-in-law, an airplane mechanic, that skill was home improvement. For you, it might be singing. It might be planning parties. It might be practicing patience with children.

Maybe your talent is craftiness, and you know how to get free things. That's another way to put more money in your pocket. I've tried to come up with some other ideas.

Get a Second Job

Sheila Schneider loves her job as a pricing analyst for a company that produces airline meals. She is twenty-five, and she is making more than $50,000 a year. "It should not be a bad salary," she said.

But it's not a great salary, given that she has $30,000 in student loans, a $300 monthly car payment, some credit card debt, grocery bills that seem to be going up, and rent that definitely is going up. "I can survive on my one paycheck, but it's very, very difficult. It's very, very tight," the Reston, Virginia, resident said.

In December 2008, she decided to take a second job. Two nights during the week and on weekend days, she works as a personal shopper at a clothing store, earning $9 an hour plus commission.

Sheila is one of many Americans supplementing their incomes with part-time or odd jobs to cope with the recession. In a survey of 1,400 workers by the staffing firm Express Employment Professionals, 42 percent said they were looking for a second job to make ends meet. In a Pew Research Center survey of 2,413 adults, 24 percent said they or someone in their household has taken an extra job because of economic troubles.

Staffing agencies across the country have seen an uptick in the number of people seeking evening and weekend jobs, even if they are overqualified for them. Traffic has increased for websites such as SnagAJob.com that specialize in hourly work.

"I think a lot more people are open to just doing any

kind of job, maybe not specifically in the field they have been trained for," said Amy Little, branch manager of Manpower, a national staffing agency. "They will just do anything and everything to make ends meet."

Second jobs don't have to be traditional, said Mechel Glass, director of education for Consumer Credit Counseling Service of Greater Atlanta. Take on sewing projects, tutor students, cook for coworkers for a fee. If you sing, try to get gigs at weddings. If you like animals, walk dogs or pet-sit.

If you love to shop, get a job with your favorite retailer. That way, you'd have the added benefit of getting discounts. If you know about traveling, electronics, movies, or just about anything, you can write a review for www .reviewstream.com. Consider direct selling at companies such as Avon, the cosmetics manufacturer.

Then, there's always self-employment.

Ron Cooper Jr.'s reason for starting a business was that the one he has been in for eleven years is in trouble. In late 2008, the Fredericksburg, Virginia, car salesman started the Stafford franchise of the national pet-waste-scooping business DoodyCalls.

"Obviously, in the auto business sales have declined over the past few years," the thirty-two-year-old said. "I felt it was a good time to try something new with a small business."

In evenings, he does advertising and bookkeeping. On Mondays, his day off from his full-time job, he scoops clients' yards. Overall, he devotes about fifteen hours a week to the business.

He's counting on this: People might stop buying Corvettes, but they will always need to have their yards cleaned.

Working a second job doesn't come without some risks, however.

"There's no question that there are times when you have conflict, especially if you take a seasonal job," said Robert Trumble, professor of management at Virginia Commonwealth University and director of the Virginia Labor Studies Center. "Most people recognize that their secondary job is secondary. But you do have to recognize that you have moments of clear conflict. Maybe both [employers] are asking for overtime and you can't do it."

Beware of the secondary costs of taking on extra work. Let's say you have children. A second job could require you to spend more on child care. Or you might have to pay more for transportation. Maybe the extra income will bump you into a higher tax bracket. How much would you have to make to cover the spread?

Juggling two jobs has certainly been a challenge for Sheila.

"I have to leave my full-time job on time. I can't put extra hours in so I can make it to my part-time job," she said.

And she doesn't have as much time to spend with her family or friends. Nor is she sleeping as much as she used to. But she is happy to have the extra income so she can pay her bills and indulge every once in a while. "I didn't want to never have spending money, to never go out with friends or see a movie," she said.

Clip Away

Thirty-four-year-old Erin Gifford has a laundry basket in her Ashburn, Virginia, home filled with toothpaste, Jell-O, and Cheerios that she got free.

No, she didn't steal them. She is a coupon master. Remember coupons? I used to clip them out of the newspaper every Sunday for my mom. I haven't thought about coupons for years. But the coupon has made a comeback.

Eager to lure customers into stores, many merchants are not only offering more coupons. They are delivering them in more creative ways, such as text-messaging them to cell phones. Consumers, meanwhile, are becoming savvier about finding good deals thanks to websites devoted to coupon-clipping.

"Marketers tend to send more coupons or issue more coupons during an economic downturn, and consumers redeem more," said Peter Meyers, vice president of marketing for ICOM Information & Communications, which conducted a survey on coupon usage. "Both are motivated. Marketers want to get more revenues, and consumers are motivated to get more savings."

Many companies such as Pillsbury and General Mills have created coupon galleries on their websites. Grocery store chains that in the past relied on their in-store circulars to advertise specials are now making their coupons available online. Some manufacturers have even banded together to offer each other's coupons on their websites, as long as the products don't compete. On BettyCrocker.com, for instance, you can find coupons for Energizer products.

It's not just groceries either; increasingly, people are using coupons for DVDs, electronics, even services such as oil changes. Clothing store chains and department stores e-mail coupons to any customer who has ever let a cashier type in his or her e-mail address. I get more e-mails from Neiman Marcus than I do from my sister.

Plenty of websites, such as CouponMom.com and CouponCabin.com, offer tips and/or spot good bargains. You can also try to get your Sunday newspaper early to study coupon offerings. Consider scouring eBay for coupons. Shoppers often exchange coupons that way. Remember to check store receipts or the product boxes themselves, for they often come with coupons.

Will Clean for Housing

Twenty-three-year-old Pari' Wright lives rent-free in suburban DC, where rents are among the highest in the nation. Her secret: Bartering.

Exchanging goods and services in lieu of cash is an antiquated system of conducting business, but in these tough economic times, it too is making a comeback. If you've got time, possessions, skills, creativity, or all the above, consider bartering. In 2007, Pari' placed an ad on Craigslist seeking a metro-accessible house or apartment. Having grown up working for her mother's house-cleaning business, she offered to clean for anyone who gave her a place to live for free.

An older woman who happened to be a pack rat responded. The woman had a basement apartment in her Northern Virginia house with a full kitchen, bathroom, and laundry facilities. "My apartment is pretty damn nice," Pari' said proudly.

It turns out that Craigslist has an entire section on bartering under the For Sale category. Curious, I logged on and found these among the posts: "Have drumkit/laptop need," "Body Piercing service and jewelry in a professional studio for barter!" and "Will help you move for your unwanted items."

There are plenty of other websites devoted to bartering. On Swaptree.com, people trade books, DVDs, and CDs and only pay for shipping. Textswap.com lets college students trade textbooks. You can swap pretty much anything on U-Exchange.com.

Since moving into the older woman's house, Pari' has bleached the walls, washed the carpet, and cleaned the yard. Next, she plans to redecorate the house. "There's a lot more people out there than you think who have needs for random things but they're not necessarily willing to pay the money," she said.

Pari' has never had a full-time job. She models when she can and works part-time at Starbucks. Thanks to her craftiness, her only real expenses are her cell phone bill and her recreation center membership. "I got a lot of skills growing up," she said. "I'm not exactly the sit-at-your-desk kind of girl. You just have to think outside the box."

But bartering could go wrong unless the arrangement is not well planned and communicated. If you're going to barter, you should use the following tips offered by the University of Illinois Extension.

Be explicit with the details. If you're trading a service

in exchange for something, make sure both parties know who will supply the required materials. Also be clear, in a contract, on payment, deadlines, and expectations.

If you are the one providing the service, make sure you actually do it well and keep the other party apprised of your progress. If there is going to be a delay, let him or her know right away.

Keep in mind that any income you receive from the trade could be taxable. IRS Publication 525, Taxable and Nontaxable Income, or your accountant should help you determine that.

If you're the one receiving the service, check the other party's qualifications. Carefully explain what you want and supervise the work.

For Sale

My friend and coworker Deborah came up with a brilliant idea for paying down some of her credit card debt. She had several pieces of gold jewelry that she stopped wearing years ago. They had no sentimental value, but plenty of monetary value.

She got online and found Goldmans, a Michigan-based company that travels around the Midwest and Mid-Atlantic region buying gold from people. When Deborah heard that the company would be in a DC hotel one weekend, she took all her jewels and sold them for almost $1,000.

As she told me this story, I thought of all the gold jewelry I had stashed away in a compartment of my jewelry box. A few months later, Goldmans returned to DC. On a Sunday afternoon in early December 2008, I grabbed a ring and several necklaces that I had not worn in years. I threw them into a small velvet bag and drove down to the hotel.

Security guards stood at the entrance of the conference room where Goldmans' employees were weighing jewelry at four separate tables. After filling out a form, they let me enter the waiting area where about a dozen people sat quietly waiting their turn. I too sat in silence, listening to the Christmas carols in the background and detangling my chains. I had not actually taken a good look at them when I gathered them that morning. One charm was emblazoned with the face of the Virgin Mary. Another was in the shape of a crucifix.

That's when the guilt crept in. I was raised Catholic but I was no longer practicing. Still, could I bring myself to sell the Virgin Mary AND Jesus? Wouldn't this assure me a place in hell?

After about an hour, a security guard gestured for me to get up. He pointed to one of the tables. I sat down in front of a smiling blonde woman.

"Hi my name is Kristin," she said.

I introduced myself. Then I handed over the jewelry. That is, except for the crucifix. That one I put back in the velvet pouch. The Virgin Mary charm, I left on the table. Selling Jesus would be unforgivable, I thought. I could probably redeem myself for selling the Virgin Mary.

Kristin picked up each piece, examined it with a magnifying loupe then weighed it.

"How's business these days?" I asked.

Booming, she said, so much so that the company was

going to spend several weekends in DC. "It's working for us," she said.

That was not surprising given that the average price of gold had more than doubled from $400 to $900 in five years. There are many other companies such as Goldmans that are taking advantage of the skyrocketing value of gold and the free-falling fortunes of indebted Americans.

Kristin weighed the pieces, wrote a bunch of stuff down on a sheet of paper, tapped away at her calculator, then offered me $228.35.

"Does that sound good?"

"Perfect," I said. I took the sheet of paper to the cashier and walked away with a check.

I still had a nagging feeling that I should not have sold the Virgin Mary charm. I consulted with Deborah the following day. She too had felt guilty as she contemplated selling a gold coin with Koranic phrases engraved in it. She decided to sell it anyway.

"God doesn't need gold," she assured me.

And we probably don't need all the unused items we have lying around our homes. If you're looking for ways to make money, dig through your closets, your shelves, and your cabinets. You can sell just about anything—clothing, china, furniture, books, DVDs, electronics—on eBay or Craigslist, both of which have had an astronomical increase in listings thanks to the economic downturn.

When you go the online route, remember that how you present your item is important. Post good photos. Describe the item with as much detail as you have, but don't write a tome that will drive people away because no relevant information appears until the third paragraph. Be honest. Remember, a lot of these websites let buyers post feedback on sellers. You don't want to get a reputation as a bad seller. Set a reasonable price or minimum bid. It would help to look at what people are paying for similar items. And don't forget to factor in shipping costs.

Consignment and thrift stores are also good options, especially if you don't want to pay for shipping or deal directly with customers. Be sure to understand the rules of whatever store you choose. Generally, consignment stores will either buy the item outright from you or pay only if the item sells. If the item is consigned, you split the final selling price with the store. Usually, you get a 40 to 60 percent cut. The store will most likely stop trying to sell the item after 90 days. Thrift stores usually take donated goods, though they also can operate on a consignment basis.

For those of you who don't want to get online or hit your local pawnshop, you can always hold an old-fashioned garage sale. If you do that, though, make sure you come up with some catchy signs.

For Rent

Who says you have to sell what you have? Why not just rent it out?

As I was asking around for ideas on making money, I came across Zilock.com. Back in fall 2007, some guys in France were trying to hang something up on a wall and didn't have a drill. They didn't want to buy one because they knew they would use it only a handful of times in their lives. Somehow they calculated that the average drill is used only an average of twelve minutes in a lifetime.

"We were thinking about all of the drills lying around the building or the block and we had no access to it. We thought there are so many ways you can sell your things online but no way to borrow things," said Jeff Boudier, one of the founders.

They launched their peer-to-peer renting website in France and Belgium. Once it took off, they expanded to the United Kingdom and the United States. Jeff, who is the U.S. general manager, said there are now 100,000 items for rent just in America. Not only are there drills up for grabs but infant cars seats, camping gear, and digital cameras. To prevent fraud, users have to register. The owners of the items set the price, and the renter has to pay a deposit. Both parties sign rental agreements.

For all you traditionalists out there, renting can be as simple as having someone pay for the use of your home while you are on vacation. I tried it in January 2009.

It didn't take long for DC's hotels to sell out for Barack Obama's historic inauguration. Those who didn't act quickly enough to reserve their rooms were left frantically searching for alternatives. To ease the housing crunch, many DC residents opened up their homes—for a price.

When one of my friends managed to rent her house during inauguration week for $3,000, I decided to advertise my apartment. I posted it on Craigslist for $500 a night. My place would be empty anyway as I was scheduled to be at a wedding in Miami the weekend before the inauguration.

By the time I got around to advertising my place, Craigslist was already filled with ads from other DC residents hoping to capitalize on the inauguration. I got no offers. About two weeks before inauguration, however, a friend of a friend called. He was a photographer and had not yet found a hotel room. I said he could have my place for $350 a night. He asked if he could stay for three. I wrote up a contract. He sent me a $500 deposit. The $1,050 I made covered my $348 plane ticket to Miami and my $350 share of the hotel room, plus all I spent on food and booze.

Swag Bags Aren't Just for Celebrities

I am constantly on the lookout for anything free. A high-level editor at the *Post* called me the biggest mooch in the newsroom once because I had gotten the *Post* to give me free hotel rooms at two journalism conferences. Both times, I had waited until the last minute to book a room and couldn't get one at a decent rate. Feeling bad for me, a couple of editors let me stay in the suite that they had rented to conduct interviews with job candidates. The only requirement was that I keep tidy and leave early in the morning so they could begin their work. I also pick the bars I go to based on the quality of the free munchies that come with the drinks. One restaurant across the street from the *Post* and a swanky hotel in downtown DC are two of my favorite spots because they give you a bottomless bowl of mixed nuts with plenty of cashews and almonds. (Lately, though, many establishments have recessionized their mixed nuts, going heavy on the peanuts.) I hit embassy parties because they always have good free appetizers or meals. And I never turn down a meal with a friend on an expense account.

I trolled around some social networking websites to find people who are good at getting free stuff.

Nancy Parode, a suburban Maryland mom and freelance writer, participates in online surveys at websites such as e-Rewards.com for free magazine subscriptions. The surveys range in topic and typically do not take more than 15 minutes. She gets a certain amount of money for each survey, sometimes $2.50 or $5, or a credit toward a prize. She accumulates that money or credit until she has enough for a subscription.

"I'm a complete magazine addict but I hate spending money on magazines," she said.

Jill Berry, a blogger in suburban Maryland, participates in online giveaways. In one three-month period, she entered twenty giveaways and won a T-shirt from MeTime.com, a $50 gift card from Wal-Mart, and a Rice Krispies treat kit from TheMotherhood.com. She scored a Nintendo DS from 5minutesformom.com.

Ryan Eubanks, a twenty-six-year-old Virginia resident, became so good at spotting freebies that he created HeyItsFree.net to share his finds. Many are toiletries such as shampoo, lotion, and toothpaste. There's also coffee, snack bars, candy, and other food items. "Freebies are a good way to tide myself over between paydays or shopping trips. I hate going to the store to buy toothpaste. I can save trips this way," he said.

Sometimes, he admits, he gets freebies he doesn't like. But that's okay. It's not like he's paying for them.

Ryan said he carefully vets the freebies to make sure they are legitimate offers. If he's suspicious, he'll check the company's domain name. He offered some other tips on weeding out bad freebie offers. Don't believe a company giving away a high-end item because high-end freebies don't exist. Don't trust a company that wants you to refer friends. Don't submit any credit card or other information beyond an e-mail address or mailing address to which the company can send the freebie. Watch for expiration dates because many companies are not good at pulling outdated offers from their websites. And if you have to do anything more than fill out a simple survey for that freebie, think twice about it.

"If they're making you jump through hoops to get the item, that's a red flag," he said.

Here are a couple of other websites devoted to helping people find freebies:

- FreeCycle.org: This nonprofit organization, whose mission is to help the environment by not cluttering landfills, matches people who want to give away items with people who want free items in the same city.
- FreeBirthdayTreats.com: Find out which restaurants give free or discounted meals and which companies give free or discounted services to people on their birthdays.
- Kidsmealdeals.com: If you have young kids, hit this site to find out where kids eat for free with a paying

adult. If you register and type in your zip code, you'll get a list of all the freebies in your area.

Okay, I had figured out how to cut costs, how to spend money more wisely, how to make money, and how to get free stuff. Now it was time for me to apply everything that I learned during all these months of financial soul-searching.

seventeen
somewhere over
the rainbow

keep thinking back to my conversation with Talia Witowski, the psychotherapist who had been a compulsive shopper while counseling addicts. Years later, she realizes that she not only deceived herself but her clients as well. That she regrets more than anything.

"I wasn't useful at all to those people," she said. "They needed a mentor and a therapist who was showing them healthy living, preaching it as well as living it, and walking the walk, and I was not that person."

Her words resonated with me. In fall 2008, I concluded that it was time to hold myself accountable for my financial failings. My planner had designed a budget for me. It wasn't so strict that I would have to give up all the things I loved in life, but it would require me to enjoy them in moderation.

I kept a diary during this time of reflection. I didn't always make the right decisions, but I was conscious when I didn't and tried to do better the next time.

WEEK 1

Hit Saturday, October 18: I'm not spending any money on meals today, I decided when I woke up. I ate at home, then went to a friend's fortieth birthday party in the evening. I bought him a bottle of Moët champagne, which is not cheap, but turning forty is a big deal. He put out a lavish spread that included caviar and smoked salmon with crème fraîche. I deducted the cost of the Moët from the very small disposable income part of my budget.

WEEK 2

Hit Monday, October 20: A colleague bought me lunch. I went straight home after hitting the gym for my spinning class. "Monday is a good night to stay in. I always stay in on Mondays," Keith once told me.

Keith is so legendary for his partying that when he moved to New York, the *New York Observer* wrote a story about his rooftop soirees in DC. If Keith can stay in on a Monday, I can too.

Hit Tuesday, October 21: I agreed to go out with an editor for another newspaper whom I had met at a journalism convention the summer before. He was on an expense account. We had drinks at the St. Regis Hotel bar then met some of his colleagues for a late dinner at a very pricey restaurant called BLT Steak. I never pulled out my wallet.

Hit Thursday, October 23: Another cheap lunch with a colleague. Another night in with an apple for dinner.

Mess Friday, October 24: Let's call this the Doggie Bag Incident of 2008.

Fridays at work are always hectic. I'm usually crashing

on deadline on a story for the Sunday business section. After having an apple for dinner a couple of nights this week, I wanted a proper meal.

Also, I had figured out a way to add on to my $100 for dining and entertainment. Christine, my planner, had budgeted $300 a month for groceries. When I dine at home, it usually consists of yogurt, granola, fruit, microwaveable soup, a sandwich, or a can of corn (I know that sounds weird but corn is delicious). Those groceries do not add up to the $75 per week that my budget allowed. I decided I would use part of that $75 to supplement my eating out.

Daphne and I met for dinner at a new restaurant. I had chicken. She had pasta. We split a bottle of wine and dessert. Knowing about the sad state of my finances, she covered the tip. Still, my half was about $40. I did not finish my chicken, so she convinced me to take it in a doggie bag. I never take home leftovers from restaurants because I usually don't eat them. "Come on. That's a good piece of chicken. Don't waste it," she insisted.

Daphne returned to our neighborhood to meet the rest of the Ontario Road crew at a bar. I stopped by a dinner party to meet a friend.

"What's that?" she and the others asked when they saw my doggie bag.

"My leftovers," I sheepishly answered.

Clearly this was not a doggie bag kind of crowd. I stayed for a drink then said my good-byes. I walked out, forgetting the doggie bag. Perhaps, subconsciously, I did it on purpose. But the host of the party noticed and called me back.

Unable to sleep, I decided to meet Daphne at a neighborhood bar. But it was too loud, so we walked out. We stood outside for a few minutes trying to figure out where to go next. Then we noticed a sign for a palm reading place next door. "Let's get our palms read," Daphne said. "Come on. It's right here. I'll pay for it."

It was $10.

"Fine," I said.

We walked in. There were two palm readers. One seemed to be in her twenties. One was much older. Both were from Romania. Daphne was taken into a separate room. I stayed out in the tiny living room, which had tattered furniture and dim lighting. The older reader studied my palm for a few moments.

"You are going to invest all your money in something big soon," she said.

"I have no money to invest," I said.

"Well, then you're going to make a lot of money soon," she said.

"Yeah, right," I said. She shot me an annoyed look.

"You are going to have three children," she said.

"I don't want any children," I said.

"You don't have a choice," she answered.

"Well, I think I do," I said.

That was pretty much the end of our conversation. Daphne's reading was just as unfulfilling. We paid and left.

"She better be right about the money and not the kids," I told Daphne.

"One more drink?" Daphne asked.

"Why not? The palm reader said I'm going to make a lot of money soon."

We slipped into Café Rumba and ordered a glass of wine each. I felt bad about letting her cover the tip for my meal and the palm reading, so I paid for our wine while she was in the restroom.

"You know, we never do that in Paris," she said when she returned and saw my doggie bag.

Then, she accidentally poked a hole in it with her finger. It was obvious, even before then, that I was not going to eat the chicken that had been sitting in a leaking Styrofoam box for three hours.

"You Parisians never leave anything on your plates to take home," I pointed out.

"The portions are smaller. Here you go to Applebee's and get an entire fried chicken for one person," she said, then laughed. "You don't even have a dog. Why do you have a doggie bag?"

"You're the one who told me to take the chicken home," I retorted.

"I was trying to prove a point," she said. "You hated carrying that box around all night. You're not a doggie bag kind of woman."

She was right. But I was wasting food and I would have to learn to either order an appetizer rather than an entrée or become a doggie bag kind of woman.

WEEK 3

Hit Monday, October 27 to Tuesday, October 28: In New York. Roy treated me to dinner Monday night. My book agent took me out for a fabulous lunch in Soho on Tuesday. An editor I know at another newspaper invited me to a book party and bought my drinks. The spread was fantastic. There were mini burgers and crab cakes. "Thank God for this," said Keith, whom I had dragged to the party. "Otherwise, I would have to buy you dinner."

I didn't pay for a single meal in New York because I either got treated by friends or business partners or I ate at my parents' house.

Hit *Saturday, November 1:* Elham and Eric had the Ontario Road crew over for brunch. I bought them orange juice and a bag of bagels from a deli in our neighborhood. It cost me about $10.

Keith came down from New York for the weekend. We went to a work party. Dinner there was free. Then we went to a Halloween party. More free food. We didn't wear costumes. I decided the cheapest thing for us to do was to all wear black and say we were dressed as the Great Depression.

WEEK 4

Mess then Hit *Monday, November 3:* I'm hating my Bug today. I had to get my registration renewed. It failed the emissions test. I got it fixed. By the end of the ordeal, I had paid $217.

That night, Daphne and I got an invite to an ambassador's house. He had a Middle Eastern buffet. We danced to Lebanese music until past midnight.

Mess *Wednesday, November 5:* Looking at my bank account today, I noticed a $34.99 monthly charge for Match.com. I had completely forgotten that in a drunken stupor with one of my girlfriends, we both signed up for Match after spending the night complaining about men. I had not gotten a single date off Match, yet I had been paying $34.99 a month for I don't even know how long. I immediately canceled it.

WEEK 5—MY BIRTHDAY WEEK!

Hits *Friday, November 7 to Wednesday, November 12:* I spent these days with the Wanderer. He paid for everything.

Thursday, November 13: The owner of my favorite neighborhood bar, Napoleon, invited me to a champagne tasting there. It was supposed to be $25 a person but he waived my cover charge.

Friday, November 14: Roy arrived from New York to celebrate my birthday with me. He covered my meals and drinks throughout the weekend.

Saturday, November 15: I bought a birthday gift for my good friend Jay. We cohosted a birthday party at Tabaq. I got gifts and free drinks all night long.

Sunday, November 16: Kavitha hosted a birthday dinner for me at her place. I know, this is starting to sound ridiculous. I tend to celebrate my birthday for days. This would go down in history as the best birthday celebration I've had thus far.

WEEK 6

Mess *Monday, November 17:* I finally paid for a dinner. Daphne, Tony, and I went out. He covered our predinner drinks, but then we decided to have a lavish meal at Central, a French bistro. This was bad: $76.99 each.

Hits *Tuesday, November 18 to Wednesday, November 19:* I wanted no more food or booze. I paid $7.21 for a slice of pumpkin loaf, a water, and latte at Starbucks and ate at home for dinner. Ditto for Wednesday.

Mess *Thursday, November 20:* I had drinks after work with my colleagues. We went to Stoney's, where the wine is not very good but cheap. We used to go to trendier places but my colleague and good friend Zach, whom I call Zee, and I decided we needed to "recessionize" our happy hours. For some reason, though, this night was expensive. I dropped $40 on dinner and drinks. I think it's because I'm usually among the last to leave. We get stuck covering for those who don't factor in tax and tip.

WEEK 7

Mess *Monday, November 24:* I was in a postbirthday, "holidays approaching with no boyfriend in sight" funk. I wanted to hang out with my friends so I wouldn't go home and play the most depressing Radiohead and Coldplay songs I could find in my iTunes collection and cry about my broken engagement, my bad hotel room breakup, and my not-so-flat belly.

Tonight, I spent $57.39 at a Mexican restaurant with a bunch of gay men. The dinner was in honor of a friend who was back in town from Iraq. The gays always cheer me up. We went to a bar after dinner for "Show Tunes" night. They bought my drinks, which was probably a bad idea. I burst into tears during "The Rainbow Connection" by Kermit the Frog. I left soon after.

Hit *Tuesday, November 25:* Shamed by my "Rainbow Connection" meltdown, I chose to have a quiet dinner with Jay. I took a bottle of wine from my kitchen collection to her place.

Personal Finance I Don't Know What *Friday, November 28:* I was in New York for Thanksgiving. My mom handed me a birthday card while I sat on my childhood bed with the same Little Mermaid comforter I used in high school. It had $60 in it. "It's not much," she said.

I felt guilty given how much she has spent on me in my lifetime. But this was her birthday tradition. I always get a card with money. "Thank you. It's too much," I said. "I love you, Mami."

Hit *Saturday, November 29:* I had a frugal Queens day. My parents, Roy, and I went to T.G.I. Friday's in Forest Hills. My dad insisted on paying. When we were done, he was in a hurry to get home. "Why do you want to leave so soon?" I asked.

It turns out that the men's room had a bathroom attendant. My dad didn't like the pressure of having to tip the attendant. But he had to use the bathroom again. "I'm not going back in there and tipping that man," he said.

He took the subway home. Little decisions like that have probably saved my dad a lot of money over his lifetime.

My sister suggested shopping. I was not going to spend money, I told myself. My sister led us into Ann Taylor Loft. My mother offered to buy us anything we wanted. "I haven't bought any clothing all year long," she said. "I need to use my credit card. My credit score isn't as high as it should be because I don't use my credit card. Can you believe that?"

"Go ahead. Be an opportunist," Roy, the little devil on my shoulder, whispered into my ear.

"No thank you, Mami. I don't need any more clothing," I said.

We walked over to the Children's Place, where she bought my nephews clothing. That was certainly a much better use of her money.

WEEK 8

Hits *Tuesday, December 2:* It was time for me to get out of my funk and get back on track with my budget. Daphne made me dinner. I took over one of the bottles of wine I had in my apartment. My friend Terri tried to get me to join her for a drink before dinner. I wanted to but declined. I needed to save the money.

Thursday, December 4: I had breakfast at home and microwave soup for lunch. I went to a book party in the evening and ate dinner there. No drinks. I was tired. I met my Financial section colleagues at Stoney's after the book party. I wanted to see them but, tired of drinking and spending money on booze, I ordered tea. Everyone laughed at me. I didn't care. My portion of the bill came to $4.

Mess *Friday, December 5 to Saturday, December 6:* I was cohosting a birthday dinner for Lizzie. Jay was cooking a curry, and I was in charge of ordering rice, naan, samosas, and cupcakes. We had asked people to RSVP. Most didn't until the day of. So I spent my day writing a story and trying to keep up with the guest list.

Then the Wanderer showed up. He had called a few days before to tell me he would be in DC for one night. He had a work-related event. We agreed to meet at the Ritz-Carlton after both of our events.

The next morning, we ordered breakfast from room service. We took our time eating. After I showered, I filled up my overnight bag with all the Bulgari sample products. The Wanderer knew of my obsession for all things Bulgari and all things free. He walked into the bathroom and opened the shower door, saying "Oh, you know what you should do?"

"I already did it," I said, knowing that he was going to suggest that I take the shampoo bottles.

"I can't believe you. Just don't take the towels, please. I'll have to pay for those," he said as he laughed.

The Wanderer left. I didn't do much that evening. The dinner party had cost me about $200. I was spent, physically and financially.

WEEK 9

Hits *Tuesday, December 9:* I had a granola bar for breakfast. For lunch, I paid $11.06 for a turkey sandwich, Cherry Coke Zero, and water.

I had a cold. I went grocery shopping after work. I spent $29.95 at the Latino grocery store near my place. I got yogurt, juice, granola bars, fruit, and some turkey. I wanted crackers too. I picked up the Carr's Peppered crackers but they were $3.69. I went for wheat crackers instead because they were $2.49. I never thought much about these things before. Now I do all the time. The Wanderer, who met me years before when I barely looked at price tags, recently told me, "Your life is an ongoing episode of *The Price Is Right.* Come on down!"

As I calculated my expenses in the evening, I watched *It's a Wonderful Life.* Life didn't seem that wonderful, I thought as I went through my budget. But there's a great scene in the movie that made me feel better. It's when Violet, the town beauty (some would say the town tramp because she was so flirtatious), asks George to lend her money so she can move to New York.

"Character...if I had any character," she says as he hands her some cash.

"It takes a lot of character to leave your hometown," he says. "You're broke, aren't you?"

"I know, but..."

"What do you want to do? Hawk your furs and that hat? You want to walk to New York?"

Violet later returns the money to George when his

uncle loses all the savings and loan's cash and he almost kills himself to avoid jail.

I kept rewinding that scene. It made me teary.

Wednesday, December 10: It's easy to not spend money when you're sick. I stayed home. I ate a granola bar and yogurt for breakfast, made my own coffee, had a banana and an apple as snacks and a sandwich for dinner.

I ended up having to write a story on my sick day anyway. Then I watched holiday DVDs.

Zee tried to get me out. I heard my friend Tony's voice in my head. "Just say no," he had told me the other day when I complained about my habit of overscheduling myself with social activities. Amit also called and asked me to join him at a holiday party that cost $40 a person.

"No," I said.

Personal Finance Checkup *Thursday, December 11:* I had a meeting with my planner.

I really wanted to go to Tryst, my favorite coffeehouse in my neighborhood, because I wanted one of their specialties, a chaippucino, but that would have required sitting down and having a waiter, paying a tip, and going through the uncomfortable "Who's going to pick up the tab?" discussion. So Starbucks it was, where Christine did indeed pay for my latte.

"How did it go?" she asked.

I pulled out the notepad on which I had penciled all my expenses. Other people use Quicken. I was still in paper-and-pencil mode. I work much better when I can see things written out in my own handwriting.

"November was great around my birthday, then it

became a disaster when I got depressed over the holidays and went to New York," I said.

"That's okay," she said. "It's not going to be perfect the first time. It's not a success or failure if you don't match it the first time. I just don't want to set you up for failure. That's why we needed to go through this. To see if we needed to readjust."

I told her that toiletries were costing a lot more than I thought they would. There was not much I could do about that, she said, except to only buy the items I need and try not to go for the expensive brands.

"It's more a budgeting item you have to plan for. I can tell you to find sales but when you need toilet paper you need toilet paper," she said.

I told her going out was still a drain on my budget. Having more dinners at friends' homes was helping. Even though I always show up with a bottle of wine or a dish, it's still less expensive than dining at a restaurant.

I asked her for advice on dealing with Christmas gifts.

She told me to make a list of all the people I have to buy gifts for and then set dollar amounts. Maybe $25, she said.

"It's the thought and gesture," she said. "When you're a giving person, you want to give nice gifts. My mother was like that."

She gave me some gift-giving ideas. Perhaps I could give someone a frame with a meaningful picture in it. Or I could make something. Or only give gifts to the children. Or do a Secret Santa.

"Have the conversation with your family," she said. "Tell them that you're on a budget."

"I had to borrow money from my parents. I think it would seem weird if I gave them flashy, expensive gifts," I said.

I brought up another problem that I had noticed: I withdraw a lot of money from the ATM and don't keep track of it.

Go to the ATM only once a week, perhaps Monday, she said. Take out $100.

"You know you have so much money in your wallet. It will deter you from getting another cash advance," she said.

She acknowledged that $100 might not be enough.

"Try it a couple of times until you get to the right number," she said.

She told me to avoid using my credit cards and to keep paying the minimum on the student and car loans, she said.

"December so far is better than November," I said.

"That's good," she said. "I like that. I'd be worried if the opposite was true. You're going in the right direction. How much do you think about money and budgeting?"

"All the time," I said.

"That's good that you're conscious of it. And that your friends are too. You're doing the right things. You need a plan for your debt. The key is living within your means. I'm glad to hear you're thinking about these things. You're taking a good first step," she said.

WEEK 10

Personal Mess, Personal Finance Hit *Tuesday, December 16:* Many newspapers across the country were cutting their staff. I was upset about not getting a raise this year but happy I still had a job.

An e-mail popped up in my Yahoo! inbox as I sat at my desk at work. "Got laid off?" it asked. It was spam but it sent me into panic mode. Suddenly, I had a sinking feeling that I could get laid off someday.

I had been planning to go home after work that night but a colleague, also upset about something work-related, asked if I wanted to have a drink at a fancy wine bar.

"I can't. I have to save my money especially if I'm going to lose my job someday," I said.

She then proposed having pizza at her place. She would pay. And she had plenty of wine.

I agreed. We text-messaged Zee and asked him to come over.

"How much longer can we do this?" I asked my colleagues as we drank our wine. Neither one of us was over the age of thirty-two. We had another forty or so years before we could retire. "I don't know how to do anything else. I can't afford law school. I should have gone into health care," I said.

We turned on the TV. The scene from the movie *Holiday Inn* in which Bing Crosby sings "White Christmas" came on. We sang along. It didn't matter that Zee is Jewish and didn't know all the words. Somehow singing "White Christmas" was making us all feel better.

I curled up into the fetal position and wondered, Which would survive the longest—the newspaper industry or my role in it?

Mess *Wednesday, December 17:* Daphne was having a dinner party. She asked me to bring berries for dessert. I went to Whole Foods. Each container was so tiny, and she said ten people would be at the dinner. I bought six plus two quarts of ice cream. Price tag: $27.03. When I showed up with the berries, Daphne looked horrified.

"Why did you buy so many? I thought you would buy two containers. I didn't want you to spend money."

"I didn't know how many containers to get. I never buy berries. I didn't know," I said.

"Oh my God, you must have spent $20 on all that," Kavitha said.

I was afraid to tell them that I had spent $27.

We were all thinking about money these days. We sat around talking about friends and relatives getting laid off. The days of pure gluttony were over. This recession was hitting all of us now. Frugality was finally in.

Daphne made me take the leftover berries home.

Hit *Thursday, December 18:* Daphne, Amit, Tony, and I had planned to have drinks and dinner. First we tried the Hotel Sofitel hotel bar. It was packed. Then we went to the Hay Adams Hotel bar. It too was packed. "I thought we were in a recession. Why is everyone out drinking at fancy hotel bars?" I asked.

Why were we out drinking at a fancy bar, we asked, after we got our bill for two rounds of drinks at the St. Regis Hotel bar. After dropping $35 for a couple of cosmopolitans each, we opted to recessionize for dinner. We would have leftovers at Daphne's.

Amit and I walked home together later that night. He had to stop by Safeway. While I waited with him at the cash register, I thumbed through the new issue of *Vogue*. Jennifer Aniston was on the cover. I love reading Jennifer Aniston stories because they make me feel better about my love life. Even a beautiful millionaire with tight abs had her heart broken. I wanted to buy the issue. But how could I justify it after canceling my *New Yorker* subscription to save money?

Amit grabbed the magazine from my hands. "It's not in our budget!"

Mess *Friday, December 19:* I was running late for my early morning C-SPAN appearance to talk about credit cards. I rushed to grab a cab. Afterward, I opted for the Metro. But walking to the station proved difficult. I was wearing a pair of black pumps with way too high heels. I really could not walk and had to stop every few minutes.

I had a choice to make. I could either take a cab home (there's no Metro stop close to my place). Or I could buy new shoes. I opted for the latter. I reasoned that I actually needed a new pair anyway since these were obviously not useful. I found one that was marked down 50 percent. I would not have gotten them otherwise. They cost $44.40.

Hit *Sunday, December 21:* I did nothing. Bought nothing. I had lunch at home and dinner at Daphne's.

WEEK 11

Hit or Mess? Monday, December 22: This was a slow week at work for a change. With the holiday approaching, my colleagues and I decided to have a proper lunch. We argued over where to go.

Choda, as we call one of our economics reporters because his name is Cho and he does a great Yoda impersonation, pushed for Old Ebbitt Grill.

Zee argued for Bobby Van's. "Lunch there is between $10 to $15," Zee insisted.

"Old Ebbitt is cheaper," Choda countered.

"But we have to take a cab there," I said. It was one of the coldest days so far this winter. Bobby Van's was just a few blocks away. We opted for Bobby Van's.

The conversation, as it always does, turned to the fate of our paper.

"Oh my God, I'm going to get laid off," I said.

No, no, no, everyone said, almost in unison.

"I'm depressed," I said. "I'm going to get laid off, and I'm fatter than I've ever been in my life."

A female colleague at our table scoffed at me. She's been on Weight Watchers since she had a baby. "You are not fat. You are always asking me for Weight Watchers tips and I refuse to give them to you."

I dug into my salad.

"All I want to do is buy a pair of boots that I can wear over skinny jeans," I declared as I recalled a pair I had seen when I had bought the black pumps.

"Don't do it," Zee said. "It's a temporary high. It's like

smoking crack but it's much more expensive and not as effective as crack. It's the stimulation of your endorphins."

Zee had never smoked crack, but for some reason was so emphatic on this point.

"Well, I've never smoked crack and don't want to. But I've bought boots and really enjoyed it," I responded.

"Buy the boots. They'll make you feel better," the female colleague said.

"Don't buy the boots," Choda said. "You'll regret it later."

"All you need is a pair of sneakers and a pair of work shoes," Zee said. "You don't need anything else."

Our lunch cost $25 each. I was definitely not going to buy boots now.

But I did need to do some Christmas shopping that night. Elham had suggested that I give people gift IOUs. "I owe you in two years," she said.

I could always regift. But I recalled a story my mom told me. She accidentally regifted her cousin a coffeemaker the cousin had given her the year before. I didn't want to take that chance.

I decided I would use neither Elham's nor my parents' approach. I would take Christine's advice and not spend more than $25 on any one gift. I stuck to it, except for my brother. That was a fluke, the result of me waiting until the last minute.

Mess *Tuesday, December 23:* In my effort to be healthy, I ended up spending $25 on lunch again. My colleagues and I once again decided to go out. We chose Logan Tavern. I originally asked for the chopped salad, which had tons of cheese and chicken in it. I thought it would have too many calories. I called back the waiter and asked for tuna and veggies. I didn't realize that the tuna was almost $20. And it was overcooked. The salad would have cost me $10.

Neither Hit nor Mess *Wednesday, December 24:* My family and I celebrated Christmas at my sister's house. Around 10:00 p.m., my nephews started getting antsy. Usually, we wait until midnight to exchange gifts. My sister let my nephews pick one gift to open before then. Seven-year-old Anthony chose the biggest box. It was a flat-screen TV.

"Ohhh, I wanted a toy. I don't want this," he whined.

"You should be grateful," my sister said.

"I don't have a TV like that. If you don't want it I'll take it," I said.

Anthony kept huffing and puffing. My sister looked hurt. (He is actually a lovely, well-behaved boy most of the time.)

"Do you realize that we are in a recession?" I asked Anthony. "Do you know how many children out there are losing their homes? You are so lucky. You have everything you need and more."

He gave me a bewildered look. I don't know why I thought I could get a seven-year-old to understand the concept of recessions and foreclosures.

Hits *Friday, December 26:* The day after Christmas can be both a dream and a nightmare for a recovering shopaholic. This year was particularly dangerous because all the stores, desperate for customers, had ridiculous sales going on. I strolled around Soho. Salespeople stood by the door handing out coupons to make customers feel like they had even more of a reason to spend money.

I almost gave in. At one store, I tried on several coats that were marked down at least 50 percent. I was so close to buying one, but then I asked myself, "Do you need another coat? Is this worth it? Do you love it? If you do and you have some cash, buy it. If not, don't bother. You will fall in love with another coat and regret buying this one."

One purchase I could justify was a couple of bottles of Kérastase, the shampoo I had been wanting for months. I found a place that had all Kérastase products discounted 30 percent. Normally, I would pay about $32 for each bottle of shampoo. I got them for $20 each.

I had dinner at Keith's. His friend cooked a Christmas feast of turkey, potatoes, squash, and other traditional dishes. We ate and danced all night.

Saturday, December 27: Roy and I met Keith and his friend for a movie. I paid for it as a thank-you for their dinner the previous night. That cost $56. Afterward, we were starving. We nixed a restaurant meal for leftovers. Turkey and stuffing taste even better the next day.

Sunday, December 28: I had Chinese food and wine with my parents. They let me have all the fortune cookies. I opened each until I found one I liked.

"Let the spirit of adventure set the tone."

Good one, but doing that sometimes leads to personal finance messes.

"To be mature is to accept imperfection."

Okay, maybe this was more apropos for the time of reflection I was going through now.

"Never chase a dog into a dead-end alley."

Hmmm, could this be about the Wanderer?

"If you want the rainbow, you have to tolerate the rain."

I liked that. I had tolerated many storms lately, but the New Year would bring me some rainbows. I could feel it.

WEEK 12

Wednesday, December 31: This was it. I was supposed to have my life in order by now. Okay, it wasn't in order but it was less chaotic.

I was on a budget. I had had some good weeks where I stayed under budget. I had had some bad weeks where I went over budget and had to cut back in some areas or stay at home for a few nights. But I had made some important changes:

I was no longer shopping for clothing every weekend to make myself feel better.

I was getting fewer manicures and pedicures.

I was eating at home more often or eating at my friends' homes.

I was openly discussing my financial situation with my family and friends.

I was paying my own rent.

I was not using my credit cards often or was sending in larger payments when I did slip and use them.

I was keeping track of my spending.

I was looking at my bank account regularly.

And when I did it, I was not afraid.

I have spent so much of my life counting calories. Now I must count money. That is the world I live in now. That is the world we all live in. Let's not call it budgeting. Let's call it being recession chic.

I spent New Year's Eve not with a lover by my side but with my best friends. Eric and Elham cooked us a feast. I brought over wine and bread. We then stopped by Kavitha's thirtieth birthday party at a bar nearby. It didn't require the $60 or $70 cover the other bars were charging. It was the nicest New Year's Eve I had had in years.

• • •

I've continued living on my budget since the New Year. I finally got part of my book advance, but I have not used it for anything but paying down a credit card. I opened a savings account to start building up my emergency cushion.

I am not perfect. I have had a few personal finance messes, like the time I decided to have a Super Bowl party just two days before the game because I got angry at a writer I was seeing for not inviting me to his condo for a small Super Bowl get-together he was having with his closest friends. I cohosted with two friends. It cost me $50 and took a lot of shopping and organizing. "This is what happens when you throw a party to spite someone," Amit told me.

But then I rented my apartment out for the inauguration weekend and made $1,050. That was most certainly a personal finance hit.

Christine told me I was pretty much on my own now, but I can e-mail her whenever I have a question. We met for coffee in early February.

"How are you doing?" she asked after buying me a latte at Starbucks.

"I'm living on my budget," I said.

But, I admitted, "I'm not 100 percent organized."

"That's still not god-awful," she said.

We looked at my objectives.

Travel. "You were still able to do it and not increase your debt," she said.

Yes, thanks to the inauguration rental.

"First step is to budget," she said.

Done.

"Second is to reduce debt."

I'm getting there, slowly.

"Third is building up emergency reserves."

I had a savings account now.

She told me not to forget my three goals: Build up my emergency funds, do not increase my debt, and have some good cash flow.

"You have a good job. You're better off than you were three months ago. You'll be better in three months," she said. "You're still contributing to your 401(k). You're on a budget. I know you wanted to be debt free but we have to take steps to get there."

"It's not perfect." I said.

"It's not perfect but life's not perfect," she said.

She's right. Life is messy.

Everyone makes bad choices when it comes to money. Look at what had happened to our economy. The financial world imploded because very smart people made very stupid decisions.

The key is to stop living in denial. Resist the urge to ignore those bills and calls from creditors. I understand how guilt and fear can leave one in a state of inertia. But it's only harmful in the end. Once you accept that you have a problem, you'll realize that there are plenty of ways to clean up those financial messes. You don't necessarily have to hire a planner to do it. All it takes is some research and long talks with friends who have made similar mistakes— and the willpower to live on a budget, to live within your means.

I've learned how to prioritize my financial obligations and wants. I can have a latte a day, but it requires cutting down on the manicures. I can still have a facial, if I eat at home a few nights that week. I can still see the world, but I don't have to go to a different country every three months.

I hope my story will prove that money, or lack thereof, does not have to ruin your life. I hope it also made you laugh at times. We have to find humor in even the saddest parts of our lives, otherwise we'll all go crazy. I hope you can apply some of the tips I have gathered so you don't have to spend sleepless nights tossing and turning. So you never again have to wonder how you can pay your rent and eat at the same time. So you never have to turn to a lover for a handout.

And just remember this: You're even hotter when you're not a mess.

appendix (for the serious stuff you need to know!)

Creating a Financial Plan

This is the first step to becoming financially stable. You can't get a hold on your finances if you don't know what you spend.

Step 1: Analyze Your Financial Health

Pull together all your important financial documents. Knowing these numbers will help you figure out your current financial health.

- Total income
- Total expenses
- Monthly net cash flow
- Year-end net worth
- Interest rates on debt and credit cards
- Marginal tax rate
- Insurance deductibles and annual out-of pocket limits

There are two basic documents you should have: A written budget (cash flow statement) and a financial statement (net worth statement).

A budget can be weekly, monthly, or annual. Follow this formula: Total income minus expenses equals net cash flow.

My Monthly Budget*		
Income	**Monthly Income**	
Wages, salary, tips		
Cash dividends and interest received		
Social security and pension income		
Other Income		
TOTAL INCOME		
Expense Description	**Target**	**Monthly Expenses**
Income Taxes		
Federal income taxes		
State income taxes		
FICA		
Emergency, Short-Term, and Midterm Savings	*10%*	
Long-Term Savings, Retirement	*20%*	
Food	*≤10%*	
Housing	*≤27%*	
Mortgage, second home mortgage		
Insurance Premiums		
Utilities: Electric, Gas, Water		
Telephone, Wireless		
Personal Services: Child Care, Adult Care		
Housing Maintenance		
Lodging Expenses, Hotels, Motels		
Housing Property: Furniture, Fixtures, Appliances, Equipment		

* All worksheets in this section are from Christine Marie Parker, certified financial planner and president of Parker Financial, an independent fee-only registered investment advisor in the state of Maryland.

Apparel	≤3%	
Transportation Expenses	≤10%	
Automobile notes		
Gas, maintenance, other		
Auto insurance		
Public transportation, air, train, bus		
Health Care	≤5%	
Health, dental, disability, long-term care insurance		
Out-of-pocket expenses, prescriptions, services		
Entertainment	≤4%	
Other Debt Payments	≤5%	
Other Expenditures		
Charity		
TOTAL EXPENSES		
= NET CASH FLOWS (Income minus Expenses)		

The formula for a financial statement is: Total assets minus total liabilities equals total net worth.

My Financial Statement (Year-End December 31, 20__)	
ASSETS	
Emergency Fund	
Checking and Savings Account	
Retirement Account(s)	
Investment Account(s)	
Value of Home	
Value of Vehicle(s)	
Value of Personal Property	
Other	

(cont.)

TOTAL ASSETS	
LIABILITIES	
Amount Owed on Mortgage	
Amount Owed on Vehicles	
Credit Card Balance Due	
Student Loan Balance Due	
Personal Loan Balance Due	
Other	
TOTAL LIABILITIES	
NET WORTH **(Assets Minus Liabilities)**	

Step 2: Define Your Goals and Objectives

Use the SMART goals system. Make your goals specific, measurable, attainable, realistic, and timely. Write down all of your goals and objectives. For each, decide if it's a "must do" or "want to do" and the time frame in which you would like to accomplish it.

My Financial Goals and Objectives		
GOALS	**Must Do**	**Want to Do**
Short-Term Goals (1–2 years)	*Ex. Accumulate emergency fund. Ex. Save and plan for a vacation.*	*Ex. Prepare an advanced directive. Ex. Save for a new/ used vehicle.*
Midterm Goals (3–10 years)	*Ex. Save for a home down payment.*	*Ex. Save for a wedding.*
Long-Term Goals (greater than 10 years)	*Ex. Save for retirement in_____.*	*Ex. Save your child's college education.*

Step 3: Figure Out How to Achieve Those Goals.

1. Decide how to spend your money. Pay yourself first. That means you should set some savings aside.
2. Prepare for emergencies. Have six to twelve months' worth of living expenses in reserves.

Step 4: Develop and Implement Your Financial Plan

Here is a good list to keep.

My Plan of Action		
Action Item	Date Due	Date Completed
Ex. Pay credit card balance off monthly.		
Ex. Save 20 percent for home mortgage down payment.		
Ex. Save 10 to 15 percent for retirement savings.		
Ex. Live within your means, spend less than your earn and stick to your budget.		
Ex. Implement a strategic asset allocation strategy for investment assets.		

You might not be able to do all of this on your own. Here are some financial institutions and advisors you should consider using:

- For banking services, consider a bank, thrift (savings and loan), or credit union. When selecting a financial institution, consider your needs (checking, savings accounts) and preferences (online banking, national access to ATMs). Compare products, fees, and benefits.

- A financial planner who can provide advice on comprehensive financial planning, tax planning strategies, investment and wealth management, and charitable planned giving. The Certified Financial Planner Board of Standards has a pamphlet titled "Questions to Ask When Choosing a Financial Planner," which is available at www.cfp.net. The Financial Planning Association offers PlannerSearch, which is available online at www.fpa.net.
- A financial broker or broker/dealer who can buy and sell securities. The Financial Industry Regulatory Authority (FINRA) offers a FINRA BrokerCheck, which is available at www.finra.org.
- An attorney who can provide legal advice and prepare estate planning documents such as wills, living wills, trusts, and powers of attorneys.
- An agent who can provide these types of insurance: life, disability, long-term care, health, auto, property, and business insurance.
- An accountant. You could complete your tax forms on your own, but if your taxes are complicated, you might want to hire a professional.

Step 5: Monitor, Reevaluate, and Revise Your Plan

Do this at least annually, for your situation might have changed or new legislation might have an impact on your finances.

Budgeting Websites*

Mint.com: This site lets you track all of your accounts:
Checking, savings, investments. You provide the
user names and passwords of all your accounts
through its secure connection. Mint will update
your accounts daily and even list your expenses
under categories such as groceries and gas.

Quicken.com: This is the web-based version of the desk-
top software. It gives you an overview of all your
accounts and even can send you a text-message
alert when you are overspending.

Thrive.com: This is a budgeting and money management
site that also analyzes your spending behavior.

Geezeo.com and *Wesabe.com:* These websites allow
you to track your expenses but they also offer an
online community. Members share their goals with
each other and create groups to share their experi-
ences and offer advice.

BudgetTracker.com and *BudgetPulse.com:* For those
who are not comfortable providing the user names
and passwords of their accounts, these websites allow
you to manually enter your financial information.

Buxfer.com: This specializes in group budgeting and
IOUs.

Additional information can be found in Chapter 4.

---

* Source: Kiplinger.com and SmartMoney.com

Filing and Paying Your Taxes*

Pull out your prior year tax return then verify your filing status, dependents, and contact information.

Next gather all these tax-related documents and forms:

All Earned and Unearned Income:
- Employee income (Form W-2)
- Income for consulting, freelancing (nonemployee income) of $600 or more will be reported on a 1099-MISC
- Retirement and pension distributions (1099-R)
- Social Security benefits (1009-SSA)
- Medical savings account distributions (1099-MSA)
- Sale of securities (1099-B)
- All interest and dividends received (1099-INT and 1099-DIV)
- Long-term care benefits (1009-LTC)
- All partnership or trust forms (K-1)
- Gambling winnings (W-2G)
- State and local tax refunds (1099-G)
- A record of all other income (i.e., alimony, rental income, etc.)

Contributions:
- 401(k) retirement plan contributions (W-2)
- IRA and Education IRA contributions (5498)

* *Source:* Christine Marie Parker, certified financial planner and president of Parker Financial, an independent fee-only registered investment advisor in the state of Maryland

- Simple and SEP retirement plan contributions (W-2 and 5498)

Tax-Related Expenses or Interest Payments:
- Mortgage interest paid (1098)
- Student loan interest paid (1098-E)
- Receipts of all qualified tax-related expenses and interest for tax deductions and credits (i.e., day care, moving, education, college, charitable donations, medical, property taxes, mortgage interest, and miscellaneous)
- All security trade confirmations
- Estimated quarterly tax payment receipts

Decide if you want to hire a professional or do your own taxes. Either way, you will have to file one of three forms:

1040 (long form)
1040A (short form)
1040EZ (easy form)

For more information, go to www.irs.gov.

Understanding Credit Cards
A credit card allows you to borrow money. You have to pay it back. Every six months, the Federal Reserve surveys the terms of credit card plans offered by several financial institutions. You can also download historical data from the semiannual survey of credit card plans, which dates back to

1990. The survey is on Form 2572. Go to www.federalreserve
.gov for this information.

When you choose a card, you have to look at several
features: fees, interest rates, and benefits. Make sure to read
the terms and conditions beforehand.

Some important terms to understand are:

Fees: These have a variety of names: annual, acti-
vation, acceptance, monthly maintenance. They
may appear monthly, periodically, or as one-time
charges, and can range from $6 to $150. They
can have an immediate effect on your available
credit. If your credit limit is $500 and you have
to pay a $100 fee, you would be left with $400 in
credit.

Transaction fees and other charges: Some companies
charge a fee if you get a cash advance, make a late
payment or exceed your credit limit.

Annual percentage rate (APR): The APR, a yearly rate
that measures the cost of credit, must be disclosed
before your account is activated and must appear
on your account statements.

The issuer also must disclose the "periodic rate." That's
the rate the issuer applies to your outstanding balance, or
the amount that you owe, to determine the finance charge
for each billing period.

Some plans come with *variable rates.* That means the
issuer can change the rate if certain economic indicators

change (if the Federal Reserve raises or lowers interest rates, for instance). The issuer must notify you if the rate could change and how the rate is determined.

Before your account is activated, you also must be given information about any limits on how much your rate may change—and how often.

> *Grace period:* You could avoid finance charges if you pay your balance in full before the due date. Without a grace period, the issuer could impose a finance charge from the date you use your card or from the date each transaction is posted to your account. You should understand what balance computation method the issuer uses. It could make a big difference in how much of a finance charge you pay.
>
> *Balance transfer offers:* Many companies offer incentives to transfer your balances to them. The most popular one is low introductory rates. But some companies charge balance transfer fees. And if you pay late or don't pay off the transferred balance before the introductory rate ends, the issuer could raise your rate and charge you interest retroactively.

Resources*

If you have questions or complaints, contact the appropriate agency.

* Source: Federal Reserve and Federal Trade Commission

Office of the Comptroller of the Currency: Regulates those banks with "national" in the name or "N.A." after the name.

Office of the Ombudsman
Customer Assistance Group
1301 McKinney Street, Suite 3450
Houston, TX 77010
Toll-free number: 800-613-6743
www.occ.treas.gov

Board of Governors of the Federal Reserve System: Regulates state-chartered banks that are members of the Federal Reserve System.

Federal Reserve Consumer Help
PO Box 1200
Minneapolis, MN 55480
Toll-free number: 888-851-1920
ConsumerHelp@FederalReserve.gov

Federal Deposit Insurance Corporation: Regulates state-chartered banks that are not members of the Federal Reserve System.

Division of Supervision and Consumer Protection
550 17th Street, NW
Washington, DC 20429
Toll-free number: 877-ASK-FDIC (275-3342)
www.fdic.gov

National Credit Union Administration: Regulates federally chartered credit unions.

Office of Public and Congressional Affairs
1775 Duke Street
Alexandria, VA 22314-3428
703-518-6330
www.ncua.gov

Office of Thrift Supervision: Regulates federal savings and loan associations and federal savings banks.

Consumer Programs
1700 G Street, NW
Washington, DC 20552
Toll-free number: 800-842-6929
www.ots.treas.gov

Federal Trade Commission: Regulates nonbank lenders.

Consumer Response Center
600 Pennsylvania Avenue, NW
Washington, DC 20580
Toll-free number: 877-FTC-HELP (382-4357)
www.ftc.gov

To compare credit card rates and offers, go to:

Bankrate.com
CardRatings.com

Credit.com

CreditCards.com

Here are some great books that discuss the ins and outs of credit cards.

Credit Card Nation: The Consequences of America's Addiction to Credit by Robert Manning (New York: Basic Books, 2000).

Credit Scores & Credit Reports by Evan Hendricks (Cabin John, MD: Privacy Times, 2005).

Maxed Out: Hard Times, Easy Credit and the Era of Predatory Lenders by James D. Scurlock (New York: Scribner, 2007).

In May 2009, President Barack Obama signed into law the Credit Card Accountability Responsibility and Disclosure Act. Most of the provisions go into effect in February 2010. Among the provisions*:

- Prevents interest rate increases on existing balances unless the borrower was at least sixty days late. The card issuers will have to restore the original rate if the borrower is on time for six months.
- Requires card companies to send a statement twenty-one days before the due date rather than fourteen days.
- Prohibits charging of interest on credit card transaction fees, such as late fees and overlimit fees.

* *Source:* Senator Christopher Dodd's website at dodd.senate.gov

- Requires that issuers give cardholders forty-five days' notice before raising the interest rate (effective August 2009).
- Prohibits anyone under twenty-one from getting a credit card unless he or she has a cosigner or can prove that he or she has the means to repay the debt.

Additional information can be found in Chapter 12.

Understanding Student Loans*

If you have federal loans, they either come directly from the federal government (the Direct Loan program) or from a private financial institution that is authorized to issue federally guaranteed loans (the Federal Family Education Loan Program, also known as FFEL). The Standard Repayment plan is a fixed monthly amount for a loan term of up to ten years.

If you can't keep up with your payments, you can suspend them through one of these two options:

- *Deferment:* You must meet certain conditions, such as being a graduate school student or unemployed or disabled. Depending on the type of loan you have, the federal government might continue to pay the interest on the loan through the deferment. Otherwise, you will have to pay the interest or add it to the balance of the loan.
- *Forbearance:* This has less favorable terms than a deferment because the interest will keep accruing,

* *Source:* FinAid.com

thus increasing the overall size of the loan. You can only do it for twelve-month intervals for up to three years. This is granted at the lender's discretion usually in cases of financial hardship.

If you don't suspend your payments, you can ask for a longer period of time to repay so that your monthly payment will shrink. Your options are:

- *Extended Repayment:* The loan repayment is spread out over twelve to thirty years to reduce the monthly payment.
- *Graduated Repayment:* This starts off with a lower monthly payment, then gradually increases every two years. It lasts between twelve to thirty years.

These are all based on income:

- *Income-Contingent Repayment:* This applies only to Direct Loan borrowers and is based on income and total debt. The monthly payment adjusts every year as the income changes. Any balance left over after twenty-five years is discharged.
- *Income-Sensitive Repayment:* This applies to FFEL loans and lasts only up to ten years. The monthly payments are a percentage of the borrower's gross monthly income.
- *Income-Based Repayment:* Started on July 1, 2009, this applies to both Direct Loan and FFEL borrowers. It caps the monthly payment at a lower percentage

of discretionary income. After twenty-five years, any remaining balance is forgiven.

Resources

AccessGroup.org
Fafsa.ed.gov
FinAid.com
Loanconsolidation.ed.gov
SallieMae.com
Studentaid.ed.gov

Additional information can be found in Chapter 12.

Car Loans
Tips for Buying a Car

1. If you can pay with cash, do it.
2. Get preapproved so you know how much money you have with which to work.
3. If not, shop around for a loan.
4. Make sure you have a high credit score. If not, try to delay your purchase so you can repair your credit.
5. Figure out how much you can afford. And don't just look at the purchase price. Consider the other costs of owning a car: maintenance expenses, tags, gas mileage, etc.
6. Decide: New or used?
7. Leasing might be an option, but tread carefully. There are pros and cons.
8. Now you have to choose a car. Do your research. Read advice columns and consumer reports. Check

the Kelley Blue Book value and websites such as Edmunds.com.

9. If you're buying from a dealership, take a friend with you to negotiate.

10. Don't let them convince you to buy unnecessary extras such as extended warranties.

11. Beware of special financing deals from the dealers. Ask about rebates instead.

12. If it's a used car, make sure you have it inspected. Get the vehicle identification number (VIN) and run a vehicle history report from CARFAX or AutoCheck to find out about accidents or thefts.

13. If you've settled for a car, shop around for insurance. Check such websites as InsWeb.com or Insurance .com.

14. If you need or want to sell the car, try doing it on your own on Craigslist. Or go to a place such as CarMax.

Resources

AutoCheck.com
Autotrader.com
Autoweb.com
CARFAX.com
Edmunds.com
Insurance.com
InsWeb.com
Kbb.com (Kelley Blue Book)

Additional information can be found in Chapter 11.

Retirement Savings

From the outset, understand the difference between tax-deferred and tax-exempt retirement accounts. With tax-deferred accounts, you contribute a portion of your salary before it is taxed. The income you make from your investments is also not subject to tax while it's in the account. Once you withdraw it upon retirement, the IRS can have its way.

With tax-exempt accounts, you contribute a portion of your after-tax income. But once you retire and withdraw that money, you owe nothing to the IRS.

The 401(k) is the most popular tax-deferred plan. But there are other kinds of accounts that fall under this umbrella. For instance, many federal government employees have the Thrift Savings Plan. They're all similar. Decide how much of your monthly income to invest in this account. Your employer automatically deducts that from your paycheck. Many employers match a percentage of your contribution—usually 50 cents on the dollar, or even the full dollar, up to 6 percent.

Choose Your Flavor

Vanguard, Fidelity, and T. Rowe Price are three of the nation's largest 401(k) providers. At the behest of your employer, this third-party administrator will let you pick among several investment types.

The younger you are, the more risk you should take because you want to beat the rate of inflation. As you get older, you should switch to more conservative investments such as bonds (also known as fixed-income because they provide investors with periodic fixed-interest payments).

Try this rule of thumb: Subtract your age from one hundred. The difference is the percentage of your portfolio to allocate to stocks.

Diversify your portfolio in order to spread that risk. Put your money in companies of different sizes and in different sectors (i.e., technology, utilities, consumer staples). Mix in some international investments. You might also be able to buy your own company's stock, but make sure you don't overdo it.

Or go with mutual funds, which are pools of investments run by professional managers. More than a quarter of Americans' retirement savings are in mutual funds. Essentially there are three types: equity (stocks), fixed-income (bonds), and money market (which invest mostly in government bonds).

Investing

If you are in your twenties and thirties, your 401(k) or similar retirement plan will contain most of your investments, in which case, you will likely have quite a bit of your money in mutual funds. If you are going to invest your money in other ways, try this*:

- Stay informed. Invest early.
- Figure out how much risk you can tolerate. Decide on your time horizon, goals, and objectives.

---

* *Source:* Christine Marie Parker, certified financial planner and president of Parker Financial, an independent fee-only registered investment advisor in the state of Maryland

- Come up with an investment plan.
- Decide on the annual return you will need.
- Strategize. Decide on your asset allocation strategy (will you have cash or invest in bonds, securities, real estate, etc.?).
- Diversify (short-, mid-, long-term; value, core, growth), and sector (financial services, health care, and technology, etc.).
- Invest in competitive well-managed companies and institutions.
- Rebalance your portfolio, at least annually.
- Evaluate fees and expenses for your investments (management fees, trading commissions, etc.).
- Monitor, review and reevaluate.

Additional information can be found in Chapter 13.

Health Insurance
Glossary

Co-Payment: The flat dollar amount you pay for medical services such as office visits. Co-insurance is your percentage share of the cost of these services.

Deductible: The dollar amount you pay out of pocket for covered services before your health insurance kicks in.

Premium: The cost of your insurance plan. If you get your insurance through your employer, you will split the premium with the company.

Types of Plans

Traditional Plan: Allows you to choose any health care provider you want, but you must pay a fee for each service you receive. You or the provider then submits a claim to your insurer for reimbursement. If the provider charges more than the insurance company is willing to pay, you make up the difference.

Managed Care Plan: Revolves around a network of physicians and hospitals with which the insurance company has negotiated rates. If you use a provider in the network, you pay less out of your own pocket. If you use one outside the network, you pay more. There are three major types of managed care plans: In an *HMO (Health Maintenance Organization)* you select a primary care physician (PCP) from a list of network providers. The PCP manages your care and refers you to specialists if needed. The HMO will typically not cover any treatment received from an out-of-network physician. With a *PPO (Preferred Provider Organization)* you don't have a primary care physician who manages all your care and decides whether or not you can see a specialist. However, even though you can go straight to a specialist if you want to, that specialist has to be within your network, otherwise you will pay a higher deductible or co-payment. For a *POS (Point-of-Service)* plan, like an HMO, you choose a primary care physician. Like a PPO, you can go to an out-of-network doctor but pay more unless the primary care physician refers you to that out-of-network doctor. You pay a higher premium.

Consumer-Directed Health Plan: These are more flexible and usually combine a high-deductible managed care plan with an account that you manage. They include the *Health Savings Account (HSA):* You and/or your employer can contribute to this account up to a certain amount. The contributions are tax-deductible and earn tax-free interest. In some cases, you can also contribute tax-free dollars from your paycheck. You can either cover a qualified medical expense with it or withdraw cash. Then there is the *Health Reimbursement Arrangement:* Your employer funds this account. Generally, you use it to pay deductibles and co-insurance under the health care plan provided by your company. In some cases, you can use it for other qualified medical expenses. You can also get *Flexible Spending Accounts,* in which money is taken from your paycheck, pretax. You can use that money for any qualified medical expense, as determined by the IRS.

Resources

Navigating Your Health Benefits for Dummies: A Reference for the Rest of Us by Tracey Baker and Charles M. Cutler (Hoboken, NJ: Wiley Publishing, 2000). PlanforYourHealth.com

Additional information can be found in Chapter 14.

Mortgages

Ask yourself a few questions:

- Does it really make sense to buy a home at this stage?
- Are you comfortable with the responsibilities of owning a home?
- Are you aware of what it costs to be a home owner?

You're ready to buy? Try this:

1. Check your credit score to make sure you can actually qualify for a mortgage with a low interest rate.
2. Figure out how much of a down payment you can afford. Again, ideally you would have at least 20 percent of the purchase price. If you have less than that, you get hit with private mortgage insurance. Another decent option if you don't have that is to get help from the Federal Housing Administration, which has a program that allows borrowers to commit as little as 3.5 percent of the purchase price. Most of the closing costs and fees can be included in the loan. Your state might also have a subsidized mortgage financing program for low- to moderate-income residents.
3. Make sure you keep abreast of tax incentives.
4. If you decide to proceed, start shopping around for a mortgage. Try multiple lenders. Get preapproved so you know what price range to look at. No more than 25 percent of your pretax income should go

toward your mortgage. Many financial advisors say you should go with a thirty-year fixed-rate loan rather than an adjustable-rate mortgage.

5. Get an agent. Recommendations from friends help. Interview a few before you settle on one.
6. Decide on a location. Look at crime statistics and the home's proximity to your work. Also consider the ease of resale. Three- or four-bedroom homes sell better than one- or two-bedrooms, for instance.
7. Make your agent negotiate. Don't be afraid to offer less than the asking price in this market.

Resources

Acorn.org

Hud.gov

Nw.org (NeighborWorks America)

Additional information can be found in Chapter 12.

about the author

NANCY TREJOS joined the *Washington Post* as a summer intern in 1998. After a brief stint at the *Los Angeles Times*, she returned to the *Post* as a staff writer in 1999, covering schools then local government. From November 2006 to January 2007, she lived in the paper's Baghdad bureau and covered the war in Iraq.

In February 2007, Ms. Trejos switched to the business section of the *Post*. She covered real estate, chronicling the bust of the real estate boom. In November 2007, she became the *Post*'s personal finance writer, writing about retirement savings, bankruptcies, and credit cards.

Ms. Trejos has written pieces for *Latina* magazine, including one about HIV-positive Latina women. She wrote a *Washington Post* magazine story about traveling to Colombia to find a half brother she had never met before.

Ms. Trejos graduated from Georgetown University with a B.A. in Government. She is originally from Queens, NY, and lives in Washington, DC.

**BUSINESS
PLUS**

Recognized as one of the world's most prestigious business imprints, Business Plus specializes in publishing books that are on the cutting edge. Like you, to be successful we always strive to be ahead of the curve.

Business Plus titles encompass a wide range of books and interests—including important business management works, state-of-the-art personal financial advice, noteworthy narrative accounts, the latest in sales and marketing advice, individualized career guidance, and autobiographies of the key business leaders of our time.

Our philosophy is that business is truly global in every way, and that today's business reader is looking for books that are both entertaining and educational. To find out more about what we're publishing, please check out the Business Plus blog at:

www.businessplusblog.com